MODERN CHINA

C. K. Macdonald

GENERAL EDITOR Jon Nichol

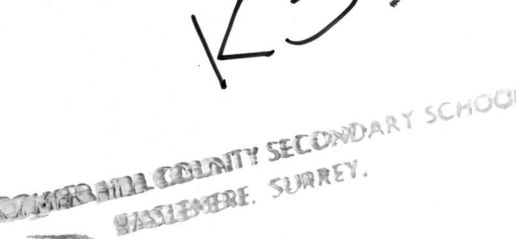

Contents

	Introduction	2	14 Changes 2	36
1	China Now	3	15 Five Year Plan: Industry 1953–57	38
2	Imperial China: Government	6	16 Farming and the Five Year Plan	40
3	Imperial China: People	8	17 Communes	44
4	The End of the Emperors	10	18 Famine!	45
5	The Warlords and the Guomindang	12	19 Communes: Two Examples	46
6	The Communist Party	14	20 Cultural Revolution 1	48
7	Massacre!	16	21 Cultural Revolution 2	51
8	The Red Army	18	22 Tibet	54
9	The Nationalist Government	21	23 China and the USSR	56
10	The Long March	24	24 The Other Chinas	59
11	China Invaded	28	25 The Struggle for Power	60
12	Communist Victory	31	26 China's Population	62
13	Changes 1	34	27 Modern China	64

SIMON & SCHUSTER
EDUCATION

Introduction

Modern China tells the story of China and the Chinese people from the 1890s to the 1980s. The book emphasises the handling of historical *evidence*. It encourages you to think actively about the clues the past has left behind. It seeks to provoke you into asking questions:

How far can this evidence be trusted? Is it *biased* (one-sided) in any way? Do I need to know more about where this evidence came from? Who wrote, spoke, drew or photographed it? Might they have a reason to hide the truth? Does this evidence support my views on what happened? If it does not, do I need to change my views on what happened?

Most of the sources in this book are *primary sources*. Primary sources are 'first-hand evidence', such as photographs, drawings, eyewitness accounts, by people who were there and witnessed what happened. The book also makes use of *secondary sources*. These 'second-hand' sources are produced by people who did not witness the event for themselves. Secondary sources used in this book include some of the newspaper reports, cartoons and accounts written by historians.

The extracts from original sources, both primary and secondary, have been adapted for classroom use where necessary.

Some of the activities in *Modern China* require you to put yourself in the position of people from the past, to face the situations they faced and to take your own decisions. This will help you to understand *why* they acted as they did and whether they took the *right* decisions. Other activities involve role-play: acting out an historical event so that you can picture it in your mind more clearly.

To begin with you may find some of the Chinese names a bit confusing. Some of them are printed at the back of the book. (You may find that older books on China spell names slightly differently. So the old spellings are also given at the back, next to the modern spellings.) In China a person's family name is always written before his or her other names. (So in Mao Zedong: *Mao* is the family name.)

You may feel that you do not know much about present day China, let alone what China was like in the past. Pages 3–5 use a modern travel guide to tell you just a *few* things about China and the Chinese people in the 1980s.

The picture on the front cover is *evidence* about life in modern China:

What is there to show that the man in the portrait is greatly admired by these people?

What does the photographer want people to think when they see this photograph?

What is there to suggest that these people are posing for the camera and that this photograph has been stage-managed?

The portrait is of Mao Zedong. He was born in 1893 into a peasant family. He went on to be the ruler of China and one of the most powerful people of all time. He helped to change the course of history.

For what purposes might this photogragh have been used?

Is it a primary or secondary source of evidence?

Teachers wanting more background knowledge about modern Chinese history may like to read *The Gate of Heavenly Peace* by Jonathan D. Spence (Penguin) from which some of the sources used in this book have been taken.

© C. K. Macdonald 1985

All rights reserved.

First published in 1985 by Basil Blackwell Ltd
Reprinted three times.

Reprinted in 1992 by Simon & Schuster Education
Campus 400
Maylands Avenue
Hemel Hempstead
Herts HP2 7EZ

ISBN 0 7501 0513 5

Typesetting by Freeman Graphic, Tonbridge, Kent
Printed in Hong Kong by Wing King Tong Co. Ltd.

Acknowledgements

Anglo–Chinese Educational Institute 40(F), 44(E), 47(D), 48(C), 52(F), 53(G), 58(K), 63(G); BBC Hulton Picture Library 6(D), 8(A), 9(G), 10(B), 17(G), 29(C); British Library 13(D); Camera Press cover, 15(D), 33(L), 42(K), 49(F); Jean-Loup Charmet 7(G); William MacQuitty 4(J), 26(E), 41(G); Magnum/The John Hillelson Agency Ltd 32(J), 35(D); The Mansell Collection 11(D); Musee Royal de l'Armee et d'Histoire Militaire, Brussels 57(D); The Photo Source 5(L), 54(A), 56(B); Popperfoto 4(F), 18(A), 19(J), 39(C), 61(F), 64(A); UPI/The Bettmann Archive 16(F), 32(F); Roger–Viollet 23(E), 28(B), 36(H).

We are also grateful for permission to use extracts from: *Fodor's China*, published by Fodor's Travel Guides (pages 3–5); and from *Birdless Summer* (pages 28–30) and *A Mortal Flower* (pages 16–17, 18–20) by Han Suyin, published by Jonathan Cape Ltd. (The passages quoted on page 16 are from *The Far East is not Very Far*, letters from Liu Yuan Lung to Anna Melissa Graves.)

1 China Now

‘*They eat all sorts of flesh, including that of dogs and animals of every kind!*’ (A)

(*Marco Polo*, a thirteenth century Italian explorer)

When did you last have a Chinese meal? In fact the food you get in your local Chinese restaurant is probably far better than the food that most Chinese people can afford. *Fodor's Travel Guide* tells us:

‘*The family meals that most people eat are simple and made from vegetables, rice and wheat. There is not much meat to be had. Pork and chicken are eaten on special occasions. Families drink large amounts of hot tea and sometimes plain hot water.*

In the south, though, it is said that people 'cook anything with four legs apart from the table'. They cook dog, cat, bear, monkey, and some types of birds' nests which they make into soup. On the coast they also eat sharksfin, turtle, eel and sea slugs.’ (B)

It is not only the food that is different. The People's Republic of China is different from Britain in almost every possible way. For a start China is a *communist* country. Since 1949 one party has ruled China – the Communist Party. You can find out what communists believe on pages 14–15. The Chinese Communist Party is very different from political parties in Britain. It does not just run the government, it controls all the important organisations in China. *Fodor's Guide* says:

‘*The Communist Party is where real power lies in China. There are about 39 million Party members, that's one in every 25 Chinese people. All key positions in the government are held by Party members. They also play a leading part in all areas of Chinese life: in the army, in schools, in farms and factories throughout China.*

Newspapers, magazines, TV and radio are all under the firm control of the Party. Through the New China News Agency the Party controls all news in China. The most important newspaper is the 'People's Daily'.’ (C)

The Communist Party strictly controls what is taught in schools. **D** shows rules used in Chinese secondary schools. In 1966 students all over China took over their schools and colleges. Most schools were closed for three years. When they re-opened some of the rules in **D** were changed. You can read more about what happened on pages 48–50. Some of the things you will learn about as you read this book are not taught in Chinese history lessons. You may be able to work out *which* things as you go along. It is unwise for Chinese people to speak out too strongly against the Communist Party. Again you will find out why later on in this book.

D School Rules

1 Aim to learn. Learn to be good in health, good in study and good in behaviour. Prepare to serve the motherland and the people.
2 Respect the national flag. Respect and love the leader of the people.
3 Obey the instructions of the Headmaster and the teachers.
4 Stand up and salute your teacher when a class begins and again at the end of the class. When you meet the Head or the teachers outside the school, you also salute them.
5 Stand up when answering the teacher's questions. Sit down when he allows you to.
6 Always arrive on time to school, and be on time for each class. Never be late, never leave the school before time and never miss a class without reason.
7 During classes sit in the correct way. Listen to the teacher carefully. Do not talk out of turn. Do not do anything else apart from your classwork.
8 Be honest and friendly with your schoolmates. Unite with them and help one another.
9 Do not smoke. Do not drink. Do not gamble. Do not take away other people's things without permission.
10 Take plenty of exercise and make your body strong.
11 Value and protect the reputation of your class and the school.
12 Always carry with you your student identity card and see that you do not lose it.

All this means that the leaders of the Chinese Communist Party are about the most powerful people in the world. There are 1000 million people living in China, that is about 20 times as many people as live in Britain, or nearly five times the population of the USA. One in every four human beings is Chinese. *Fodor's Guide* points out:

‘*China is a vast land. It is the third largest country in the world, after the USSR and Canada. But only 12 per cent of the land is really good land for growing crops. Over half the country is covered in mountains. This means that China's huge population depends on food grown in a fairly small area of the country. So the weather is all-important to the people of China. The weather can make the difference between large crops in good years and famine because of drought or floods in bad years. China is at the mercy of the weather.*’ (E)

You can find out about one of the worst famines in the history of China on page 45. **F** shows how Chinese peasants manage to farm the sides of mountains.

F Terraced hillsides in Gansu province

‘*94 per cent of the people of China are Han people. The other 6 per cent are from other races. Yet these other races live in about two-thirds of China's total land area, in Tibet, Xinjiang, Inner Mongolia and Sichuan.*’ (H)

The map at the front of this book shows where these places are. The *Guide* goes on:

‘*80 per cent of the people of China live in the countryside as peasants. Most of them live in small houses made of mud bricks with thatch roofs. Some live in newer tile roof cottages made of clay bricks. The whole family lives in two or three rooms. In most the only lighting is by oil lamp. Often the bedrooms have no windows to keep the heat in. Only the modern houses have glass windows. Peasants usually have little furniture except for a table, chairs and beds. The working day is long and hard* (see J).

J Farm machinery is rare in China

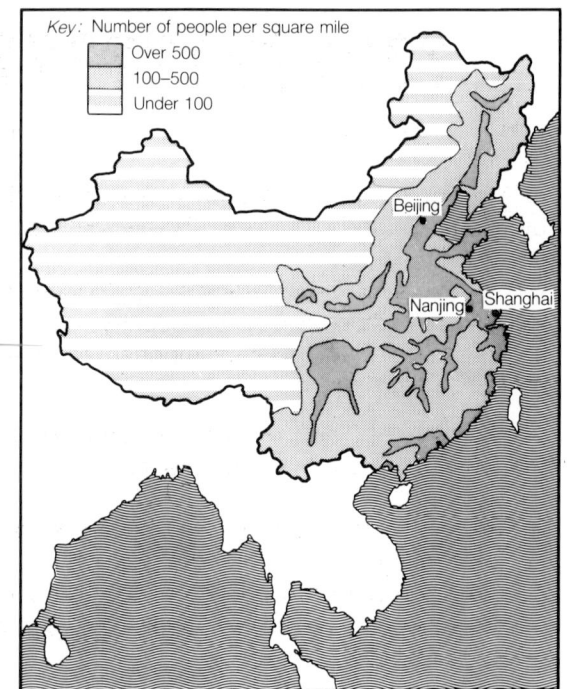

G Population density in China

G shows where most people in China live. *Fodor's Guide* says:

Town workers are better off than the peasants. They don't have to work as hard and they certainly live in better conditions. Most of them live in a small house or flat, again with two or three rooms. Families usually share kitchens with other families and they do not have many belongings. There will be few decorations, except for a print of Chairman Mao. Usually they have electricity but most houses and flats have to share supplies of running water. In some smaller towns the water is drawn from wells.

Little is wasted in China. Sewage is collected during the night by wagons and taken to treatment centres. Then it is put on the surrounding fields. Everyone who is not a student is expected to work. Families rise early, usually before sunrise. In the towns people walk, cycle or take a bus to work. There are no privately owned cars in China.*’ (K)

Women are expected to do the housework and the cooking and look after the children. Most factories have nurseries where young children can be looked after while their parents are at work. Even so, most Chinese women are better off now than they used to be. L shows a very old Chinese woman. Look at her feet. There are many thousands of old ladies in China with feet like this. You can find out why on pages 8–9.

A person's place of work is very important in China. Every Chinese citizen is a member of a work unit. This may be a factory, office, village or school. The leaders of the work unit have a lot of control over the workers' lives. If they want to buy something expensive such as a TV or bicycle they must get permission from their work unit leaders. If they want to get married they must get permission first. If a married couple wish to have a baby they must apply for permission. They are only allowed to have one child. Pages 62–63 explain why.

In the 1980s living standards in China are going up. More and more people can afford TVs. Many of the programmes are American. Chinese people are buying more and more goods from the USA and European countries. Western clothes and music are very popular in the towns and cities. The government is very worried about the effect all this is having on young people. *Fodor's Guide* says:

❛*In China all these changes are causing both excitement and worry. China's youth are becoming 'restless'. Party officials point out that they are all too interested in 'unhealthy music' and 'weird clothes', and some of them 'even wish to wriggle their bottoms when they dance'!*❜ **(M)**

Visitors returning from China say different things about what the country is like. *Fodor's Guide* warns travellers:

❛*When people visit China they end up seeing it in the way they want to see it. Some visitors come back saying: 'China is a place where people are equal, where crime does not exist and everyone has a job and plenty to eat. China is a place where people respect one another and where family life is important. Life is simple.' That's what some travellers would have us believe. Others come back saying: 'China is a place where people are put down and where people are not allowed to say what they think. Crime is low, but that is because everyone's life is totally controlled. China is a place where religion has been stamped out, where building design is dreadful, where there is not enough food, clothing and housing, and where people are slaves of the government.' That's what other travellers would have us believe.*❜ **(N)**

In China, as in any place in the world at any time, what happened in the past shapes what happens now and in the future.

L   What has happened to this old lady's feet?

??????????????

1 a Why is the Communist Party very powerful in China?
  b What evidence is there on these pages that by Western standards most Chinese people are very poor?
  c In what ways is life better for people living in the towns than for those living in the countryside?
  d Why are the work units so important for everyone's daily life in China?

2 a What do rules 2 and 4 in **D** tell us about the aims of schools in China? Do British schools try to do the same thing?
  b What kinds of things might the Communist Party not want young people to learn about in schools?
  c Why is the Communist Party so worried about young people? What does this tell us about the Communist Party?

3 Look at **C** and **N**. If *Fodor's Guide* is right, what special problems are there for the historian in finding out about China's past? How might the writers of *Fodor's Guide* have got their information? What problems are there in relying on such a guide as a source of information?

2 Imperial China: Government

‹ *China is like a large building, that because its timbers have decayed is about to fall down. If small patches are made to cover up the cracks, then as soon as there is a storm the building will collapse. It is therefore necessary to completely rebuild the building.* › **(A)**

A is from a letter sent to Guangxu, Emperor of China, in 1898. It was written by a leading Chinese student, Kang Youwei.

China had been ruled by emperors for thousands of years. Each emperor of China had complete power. He could make or change any law he wished. He was called 'Son of Heaven, Ruler of the World'. In many ways the emperor was treated like a god. However if an emperor was weak or did not rule wisely he might be overthrown, and replaced by another emperor. This had happened several times in Chinese history. The last time had been in 1644 when the Manchus had invaded China from Manchuria. Since then a Manchu family called Qing had ruled China, and the Manchus had become the richest and most powerful people in China. Even in 1898 the Manchus had different customs and often spoke a different language from the rest of the Chinese people. Chinese men wore pigtails as a sign of loyalty to the Manchus.

The emperor lived in Beijing in the 'Forbidden City', out of touch with what was going on in the rest of China. The Manchu nobility's life of luxury was very different from the lives of most people. Kang wrote:

‹ *No matter where you look in Beijing the place is covered with beggars. The homeless and the old; the crippled and the sick — with no one to care for them they fall dead on the roads. This happens every day. And the coaches of the great government officials rumble past them all the time. They don't worry any more than officials in the rest of the country.* › **(B)**

Government officials were called 'mandarins'. To become a mandarin a man had to pass very difficult examinations in Classics, the ancient learning of China. People often spent half their lives studying for these examinations. Only the rich could become mandarins because only they could afford to be educated. The ancient learning had little to do with the modern world. It encouraged officials to take pride in the old Chinese ways and to look down on all other learning as 'barbarian'.

The Chinese faced many problems. Kang wrote:

‹ *The population continues to grow. Yet our industry and trade have not grown. The people's lives have grown harder and harder. Some have emigrated to other countries — there to live as slaves. Others have become thugs who prey upon their local villages.* › **(C)**

D shows what happened to these thugs, and to many other people who broke the law, if they were caught.

Many foreigners thought of China as a 'backward' country. Yet China was a rich country in many ways. So rich, in fact, that many other countries wanted to trade with China and take a share of her wealth. For instance, Britain wanted China's tea, silk, cotton and porcelain, among other things. The only thing the British could offer in return was the drug opium. They smuggled large shipments of opium to China which led to hundreds of thousands of Chinese becoming drug addicts. In 1839 the Chinese government declared war on Britain. But the Chinese army and navy were completely out of date. The British won a crushing victory. In 1842 they made the Chinese sign the Treaty of Nanjing. This was the first of what the Chinese called 'The Unequal Treaties'. It said:

‹ *. . . His Majesty the Emperor of China agrees that British people shall be allowed to live in certain cities in China under British law.*

. . . His Majesty the Emperor of China gives to Her Majesty the Queen of Great Britain the island of Hong Kong for all time.

. . . British merchants shall be allowed to trade in China with whomever they please. ›

D Bodies of executed law-breakers lying in the streets

... The Emperor of China agrees to pay the sum of 12 million dollars to pay for the cost of the war. (E)

Other countries saw that there were easy gains to be had in China. They were quick to follow Britain's example. By 1898 China had lost Eastern Siberia and Vladivostock to the Russians, Vietnam to the French, Burma to the British, and Qingdao to the Germans. In 1895 China was easily defeated in a war with Japan. Japan had once been part of the Chinese Empire but was now the most advanced country in the Far East. In 1895 Japan took Korea and Taiwan from China. By 1900 much of China's coastline was controlled by foreign countries (see map **F**).

Under the Unequal Treaties foreign powers were allowed to sell their goods cheaply in China, without the Chinese government putting heavy duties on them. This forced many traditional Chinese industries out of business.

Foreign countries were taking control of China (see **G**). The few modern mines, factories and railways were usually owned by foreign businessmen. Even ancient Chinese religious beliefs were under attack. The Chinese government was forced to allow Christian missionaries to preach wherever they liked in China.

In 1893 Emperor Guangxu decided to act. He sent out this notice to the mandarins:

Our government officials think that we have nothing to learn

G Foreign powers share out the Chinese 'cake'

from the Europeans. They are wrong. My duty as ruler must be to give my people peace and prosperity. Foreign powers surround us. They often attack us. Unless we learn to copy the sources of their power then we can have no hope. (H)

But it was too late to save Imperial China.

F Areas of China under foreign control

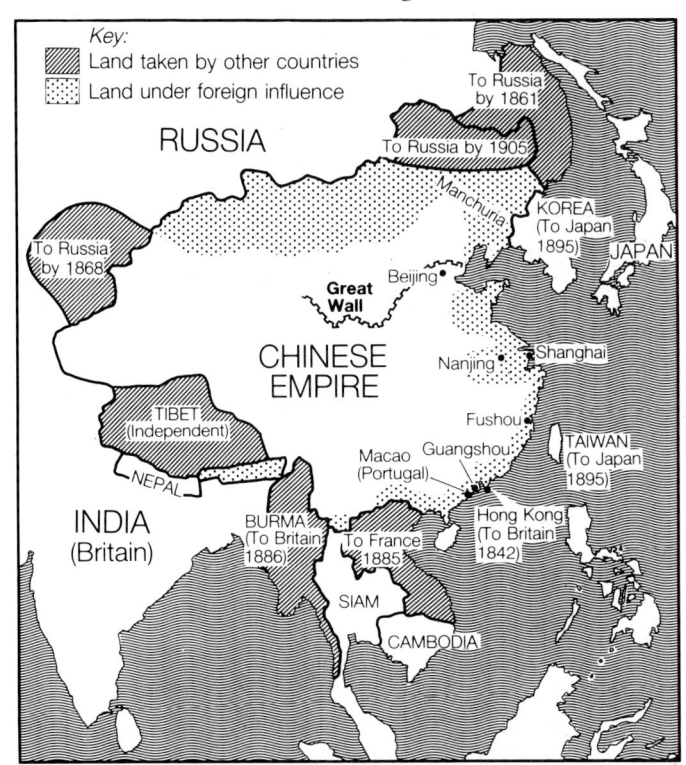

??????????????

1 a Who was Emperor of China in 1898?
b Who were the Manchus? Why were they the richest people in China?
c What evidence is there that the mandarins were out of touch with China's problems? Why was this?
d In what ways was life hard for the ordinary people?
e Why did European countries want to trade with China?
f How was the Nanjing Treaty unequal?

2 What point is cartoon **G** trying to make? Do you think it is a Chinese cartoon or a foreign cartoon? Why?

3 Either a Design your own cartoon showing some of the problems faced by China.
or b Write a letter like Kang did to the Emperor, explaining what you think is wrong with China. Suggest some changes that the Emperor might make to help solve China's problems.

3 Imperial China: People

A Some poor peasants were forced to beg for food

Most of the people in Imperial China were peasants. In good years they struggled to survive. In bad years they starved. A is an example of the kind of poverty that many peasants lived in.

The population of China was growing. By 1900 there were nearly 500 million people in China. This meant that there was not enough land to go round. Very few peasants owned their own land. Most rented their land from a local landlord. Many old people in China still have bitter memories of their landlords:

‘I came from a peasant home. I began working when I was seven. I herded cows and goats. Later I began to work in the fields. Many years later I kept hearing of revolutionaries who had destroyed the landowners and done away with taxes. That made a deep impression on me. I really liked the idea of landowners being killed because landowners lived in luxury while the people suffered.’ (B)

On top of heavy rents, the peasants also had to pay taxes. Usually these taxes were collected on the orders of the landlord. Here is a list of some of the taxes peasants in Gansu Province were paying right up until 1949:

‘Land tax, kettle tax, stocking tax, bedding tax, wheat bran tax, water-mill tax, copper tax, flour shop tax, extraordinary tax, hog tax, penalty tax, wealthy house tax, door and window tax, cleaning of the countryside tax, army mule tax, kindling wood tax, skin overcoat tax, temporary expenses tax, soldier enlistment tax, hemp shoe tax, troop movement tax, extra expenses tax, soldier reward tax.’ (C)

Most of these taxes were meant to go to the government. However, in many cases the local landowning family was responsible for the government of their area. The mandarins were usually themselves the sons of landowners. The local government, courts and police (where there were any) were controlled by the landowners. So *they* decided how the taxes were spent. Any peasant who could not, or would not, pay his taxes or rent could be dealt with in the local courts. If the landlord raised the rent or taxes there was little the peasants could do about it.

Some peasants owned their own land and were better off than others. These richer peasants would sometimes lend money to their poorer neighbours, charging high rates of interest. The poorest peasants often hated these money lenders as much as their landlords.

If peasant life was hard for men it was far worse for women. **D** is from an essay written in 1904 by Qiu Jin, a young Chinese student, while she was studying in Japan. She describes some of the problems that all Chinese women faced:

'We, the 200 million women of China, are the most unfairly treated objects on this earth. If we have a good father, then we will be all right at the time of our birth; but if he is a crude or bad man he will say: 'Oh what a terrible day, here's another useless one.' If only he could he would dash us to the ground . . . Before many years have passed, they take out a pair of snow-white bands and bind them round our feet. They then tighten them with strips of white cotton. Even when we go to bed at night we are not allowed to loosen them the least bit. The result is that the flesh peels away and the bones bend and buckle under. The only reason for doing all this is just to make sure that our friends and neighbours will all say: 'At the so-and-so's all the girls have got such lovely small feet!' (**D**)

If a woman had small feet it was seen as a mark of beauty. Often girls became crippled. Qiu wrote:

'As long as we have these tiny three-inch feet we can do nothing. We must end the practice!' (**E**)

According to Qiu, women also suffered in other ways:

'When it comes to picking a son-in-law, parents usually only care that the man's family have money or influence. They don't bother to find out what he is like as a person, or whether he is bright or stupid. Once you are married, as long as your husband turns out to be a family man they will say you are blessed. They will say that you must have been blessed in one of your previous lives and are being rewarded in this life. If he turns out to be no good people will say that you are being punished for the things you did wrong in a previous life.' (**F**)

As Qiu suggests, many Chinese people believed that they had lived before. **G** shows a village temple, in which local peasants worshipped village gods and also their own ancestors.

Each year thousands of peasants left their villages and moved to the towns, hoping for a better life. Usually they ended up as *coolies*, working for very low wages. (Coolie come from the Chinese 'ku-li', meaning bitter strength and work.)

H was written by a man called Zou Rong in 1903. Zou believed the only answer to China's problems was revolution. He was not the only one:

G A village temple

'You the Chinese people possess government – run it yourselves. You have laws – guard them yourselves. You have industries – own them yourselves. You possess armed forces – order them yourselves. You possess lands – watch over them yourselves. You have an endless supply of natural resources – use them yourselves. You are ready in every way for revolution.' (**H**)

Zou was put in prison for writing this. Conditions in prison were so bad that he became ill and died within two years. He was 19 years old.

By the time Zou died China was in a bigger mess than ever. The Emperor had tried to bring in changes, but these had gone badly wrong, as the next section shows.

??????????????

1 a Why was there not enough land to go round?
b What evidence is there in these pages to show that many peasants hated their landlords?
c What might the people in **A** tell you about their poverty?
d Why were the landowners so powerful?

2 Use **D**, **E** and **F** to explain how women suffered in Imperial China. Are there any similar ways in which women are 'maltreated' in our society?

3 How far can we trust **B**, **C**, **E** and **F** as reliable sources of evidence? Which are primary sources and which are secondary sources?

4 In groups work out a list of measures that the government of Imperial China might take to help:
 a peasants
 b women
Compare your suggestions. If the government tried to put these measures into effect what might happen? Do you think Zou Rong was right in saying that revolution was the only way to make real changes in China (see **H**)?

4 The End of the Emperors

The Emperor wanted reforms in China but his aunt the Empress Dowager did not. Empress Dowager Cixi had ruled China when the Emperor was a boy and too young to rule by himself. She was still very powerful. On 20 September 1898 she gave orders for the Emperor to be arrested. Six of the reformers, including Kang's brother, were arrested, tried for treason and executed. The Empress Dowager now ruled alone. All attempts to bring about changes in China ended.

In 1900 the Empress Dowager gave her support to an uprising called the 'Boxer Rebellion'. The *Boxers* were a secret society who believed they had special magic powers. A Boxer poster that was stuck up in Shandong provides evidence of their aims:

❝*We are forced to practise magic boxing to protect our country. We will expel the foreign robbers and kill the other devils (Chinese Christians). So that our people may be saved from suffering, get rid of any devils that live in your village. Burn down all their churches. Anyone who tries to disobey this order by hiding Christians will be burnt to death. You have been warned.*❞ (A)

Thousands of Christians were killed. Railways, factories and post offices were destroyed. When the Boxers entered Beijing they killed several foreigners, including the German Ambassador. The Western powers and the Japanese decided to act. European and Japanese forces marched on Beijing. Cartoon **B** is about how they dealt with the Rebellion.

The Empress Dowager fled from Beijing, taking the Emperor with her. She was only allowed back into the city when she agreed to allow foreign soldiers to be stationed there. China was also made to pay the cost of putting down the rebellion.

Things were made even worse when floods destroyed crops in China. Millions of peasants starved. Many Chinese people felt that their government had failed them once again. Support for revolutionary groups grew. One of these groups was led by Dr Sun Yatsen. Sun Yatsen was a nationalist. He wrote:

❝*We have been invaded by foreign forces and their control of our economy makes us like prisoners. Now we are unable to fight back. If we want to save China, if we wish to see the Chinese race survive forever, we must preach nationalism. What is the standing of our race in the world? When we compare all the races in the world, we see that we are the*

B One artist's view of how the European powers crushed the Boxer Rebellion

biggest in number, that our race is the greatest and that our history dates back more than 4000 years. But if we do not join together into one strong race, China will be destroyed as a nation and will die! **(C)**

Sun Yatsen wanted China to become an industrial country, like Japan. The Japanese had grown so strong that they were even able to defeat mighty Russia in a war in 1905. In 1907 Sun started revolts in several parts of China. They all failed. Sun was forced to leave the country.

In November 1908 the Emperor, still a prisoner, died. The next day the Empress Dowager died as well. The new Emperor, Puyi **(D)** was three years old. Now the country had no strong leader. In addition, poor harvests and outbreaks of disease brought more hardship and poverty for the Chinese peasants.

In October 1911, during a police raid on a building in Wuhan, a list of Sun Yatsen's supporters was found. Many of the names on the list were Chinese soldiers stationed in Wuhan. When faced with arrest the soldiers rebelled. They took control of the city and thousands joined them. The revolt spread quickly and soon much of the south was in rebel hands. All over the south men cut off their pig-tails as a sign of defiance. In some areas there was a lot of bloodshed. A young boy in Fenghuang called Hunan later wrote down his memories of the revolution:

D Emperor Puyi

'The building was covered with heads. I was amazed and did not understand why all these people had been killed. Not long after I found a string of ears, a strange sight that not many see in a lifetime. Why had they been beheaded? I was uncertain and when I returned I asked my father. His answer was 'revolution', which was not a satisfactory answer at all.' **(E)**

Sun Yatsen was in the USA when he heard the news. He hurried back to China. On his return huge crowds cheered him through the streets of Shanghai.

An assembly of rebel leaders was held. Sun Yatsen was elected 'Provisional President of the Republic of China'. However, northern China was still in the hands of the imperial government. General Yuan Shikai, head of the Imperial army, was sent to put down the rebellion. Instead, Yuan betrayed the government and made an agreement with Sun Yatsen. They decided that Yuan and his army would join up with Sun and force Emperor Puyi to *abdicate* (resign). In return Sun agreed that Yuan should take over as president of the new China.

On 12 February 1912 Emperor Puyi abdicated. Yuan became President of the Republic of China. After thousands of years it was the end of the emperors.

??????????????

1 a What does the evidence in these pages tell us about the character of the Empress Dowager?
b What were the aims of the Boxers?
c How was the Boxer Rebellion ended?
d Why did support for the revolutionary groups grow?
e Why was Sun Yatsen forced to leave the country?
f What problems did the government have after the deaths of the Emperor and Empress Dowager?

2 Use the evidence in **C** to explain what a *nationalist* is.

3 As though you are a revolutionary, write a telegram to Dr Sun Yatsen telling him about the events of 1911. Mention: soldiers in Wuhan, the fighting, your wish for Sun to return to China, what you think will happen now.

4 a Which of **A–E** are *primary* sources and which are *secondary* sources? Are there any that you are not sure about? Why not?
b Look at **B**. Do you think it is: a European cartoon; a Chinese cartoon; or a Japanese cartoon? Give reasons for your answer.
c How far can we trust **B** and **E**?

5 The Warlords and the Guomindang

Sun Yatsen hoped that with the Emperor gone things would get better in China. In 1912 Sun and other nationalists formed the *Guomindang* or National People's Party. The Guomindang had three main principles, (**A**).

A The three main principles of the Guomindang

> **Democracy** A parliament should be freely elected, as in Britain, to run the country. A constitution or set of rules should be written to stop the government from having too much power.
>
> **National unity** All Chinese people should be united into one strong country. All foreign interference in China should be ended, by force where necessary.
>
> **People's welfare** Everyone in China should have basic food and shelter. The government should help provide this and also take control of key industries such as the railways and mines.

But Sun's hopes were soon to be dashed!

Democracy

In 1913 a Parliament was elected in China. The Guomindang won most seats. It looked as though Song Jiaoren, a leading member of the Guomindang, would become Prime Minister. On 20 March 1913, as Song was about to get on a train at Shanghai station to go to Beijing, he was shot dead by a hired gunman. President Yuan Shikai had ordered the killing. When the Guomindang tried to start an uprising against Yuan he banned the party. Yuan's army then seized Nanjing, the main centre of Guomindang support. Hundreds of Guomindang members were killed. Sun Yatsen was forced to leave the country for a while. Yuan now closed the Parliament and tried to rule the country through the army. In 1915 he even tried to make himself emperor.

National Unity

However Yuan's power was slipping away. All over China generals and bandits were seizing parts of the country for themselves. These *warlords* fought with each other for control of China. Many of the warlords were brutal men. They used their armies to hunt down anyone they suspected of being against them. Millions of people lived in fear.

The Japanese government saw its chance to increase its power in China. In the First World War (1914–18), Japan fought on the Allies' side, against the Germans. In 1915 the Japanese invaded Qingdao (see map inside front cover), which the Germans controlled. The Chinese government was forced to accept '21 Demands' from the Japanese. These included:

> *1 Whenever the Chinese wish another foreign power to help build a railway in South Manchuria or Eastern Mongolia they must get permission from Japan.*
> *2 Japanese officials shall hold important positions in the Chinese government to help advise on political, military and money matters.*
> *3 At least half of all weapons bought by the Chinese government must be made in Japan.* (**B**)

When Yuan Shikai died in 1916 government in China broke down completely.

Perhaps the greatest blow to Sun's hopes came from Britain, France and the USA in 1919. The Versailles Treaty at the end of the First World War upheld Japan's 21 Demands. A young man called Qu Qiubai, who later became a communist, wrote:

> *The taste of colonialism (foreign control) in its full bitterness had never come home to the Chinese until then, even though we had already had the experience of tens of years of mistreatment by foreigners. The sharp pain of foreign empire-building in China then reached the marrow of our bones.* (**C**)

On 4 May 1919 students in Beijing protested against the Versailles Treaty. Fighting broke out and the police took action. Several students were wounded, others ended up in prison. A group of students now formed the 'Fourth of May Movement'. They gave their support to the Guomindang.

People's Welfare

Millions of ordinary people died as the warlords fought each other. Some were killed in the battles. Others died of starvation. In 1920–1 there was a terrible famine in northern China. No one knows how many people died.

Sun Yatsen had set up a new government of his own in Guangzhou. He realised that if his three principles were to be achieved the Guomindang would have to conquer the country first. There seemed to be little chance of this: Sun's government could only exist at all as long as he did not upset the local warlord.

After the Versailles Treaty Sun felt that he had been

D The Northern Expedition

betrayed by the Western democracies. He turned to the USSR (Communist Russia) for help. He sent his top general, Chiang Kaishek, to Moscow. By 1923 the Russians were supplying the Guomindang with money, weapons and advisors. In 1924 the Guomindang made an alliance with the newly formed Communist Party of China (see pages 14–15).

By the time Sun Yatsen died in 1925 the Guomindang was fighting back. Chiang Kaishek made himself the new leader of the Guomindang. He felt his forces were now strong enough to start a major attack on the warlords. Chiang's 'Northern Expedition' began in 1926. **D** is a poster showing Chiang's forces in action. They were very successful.

While Chiang fought the warlord armies, the communists, such as Mao Zedong, organised strikes by workers, peasant uprisings and demonstrations in support of the Guomindang. The warlords used every means to crush them. A strike by the General Labour Union in Shanghai in 1927 resulted in 20 strike leaders having their heads cut off. A Beijing teacher, Lu Xun, described in a letter to a friend what happened to some of his pupils when they took part in a demonstration (**E**). The Guomindang and the Communist Party had organised the demonstration against the local warlord Feng Yuxiang:

'On the morning of the 18th I knew there was a mass demonstration before Government House. That afternoon I heard the fearful news that the guards had actually opened fire, that there had been several hundred people hurt and that Liu Hezhen (one of his pupils) was one of the dead.

... Liu Hezhen went forward happily. Of course it was only a protest and no decent person could imagine there might be a trap. But then she was shot – shot from behind and the bullet pierced her lung and heart ... When Zhang Jingshu ... tried to lift her up, she too was hit – four shots. And when Yang Dezhun who was with them tried to help she too was shot and fell. She sat up, but a soldier clubbed her over the head and so she died ...' (**E**)

By now the days of the warlords were numbered. Their soldiers deserted in thousands to join the Guomindang. By early 1927 Chiang controlled most of China south of the Yangtze River. Meanwhile communists led by Zhou Enlai were helping to take over Shanghai, a city long ruled by foreigners. The alliance between the Guomindang and the communists seemed to be working: together it seemed they would conquer all of China.

Chiang Kaishek had other plans. He was worried that the communists were becoming too strong, and that they were getting too much support from the peasants and workers. He also disliked Mao Zedong's political ideas and those of other communists (see pages 14–15). Chiang wanted a united China and a strong China, but he did not want a communist China. Early in 1927 a young student noted:

'The troubles caused by the reds (communists) are violent and wild. This puts a heavy burden on the nationalists. Progressing at all will get harder and harder. In the very near future there is going to be a violent battle between communism and nationalism.' (**F**)

??????????????

1 a In what ways did Yuan Shikai betray Sun Yatsen?
b How did the warlords rule the areas they controlled?
c Which of the demands in **B** do you think that members of the Guomindang hated most?
d What was the 'Fourth of May Movement'?
e Why did Sun turn to the USSR for help?
f How did the Chinese Communist Party help the Guomindang during the Northern Expedition?
e Why do you think the warlords dealt so harshly with protests and strikes?

2 What is there in **E** to suggest that Lu Xun had probably spoken to an eyewitness of the demonstration (rather than simply reading about it in an illegal newspaper)?

3 Imagine you are a member of the Guomindang in 1927.
Either **a** design a leaflet aimed at getting people to support the Guomindang. (Think about: Sun Yatsen's Three Principles; warlords; 21 Demands; starvation; the Communist Party; Chiang Kaishek; Northern Expedition; strikes; demonstrations.)
or **b** Design a poster like **D** supporting the Guomindang.

6 The Communist Party

*❝Imagine no possessions, I wonder if you can!
No need for greed or hunger, a brotherhood of man.
Imagine all the people sharing all the world.*

*Imagine there's no countries, it isn't hard to do.
Nothing to kill or die for and no religion too.
Imagine all the people living life in peace.*

*You may say I'm a dreamer but I'm not the only one.
I hope some day you'll join us.
And the world will live as one.❞* (A)

This song was written by the ex-'Beatle' John Lennon. It describes the kind of society that most communists want to bring about. Communist parties exist in nearly every country in the world. Half of the people in the world, including the Chinese, are now ruled by governments claiming to be communist.

Communists get their ideas from the German writer, Karl Marx. His most famous book is the *Communist Manifesto*, written in 1848. In it Marx wrote:

❝*Communists everywhere support every revolutionary movement against the existing order of things. The communists do not hide their views and aims. They openly say that what they want can only be achieved by force. Let the ruling classes tremble at the workers' revolution. The workers have nothing to lose but their chains! They have a world to win!*
WORKING MEN OF ALL COUNTRIES, UNITE!❞ (B)

Table C sets out Marx's ideas. When Marx died in 1883, his ideas were already spreading. In 1917 there was a revolution in Russia. Communists, led by Lenin, seized power. Russia was a poor and backward country in which most of the people were peasants. It was not at all the kind of country Marx had expected to have a communist revolution. However, some Chinese people thought: if it can happen in Russia it can happen in China. One of these people was Mao Zedong (D), the future leader of China. He later wrote:

C

MARXISM

Marx believed that all human history is a struggle for power between those who own society's wealth and those who do not. It is a struggle between different *classes* of people – between the 'Haves' and the 'Have-nots'. Marx argued that *all* societies go through three main stages in their history: *Feudalism, Capitalism* and *Communism*.

Stage 1 Feudalism: In a feudal society the main way of earning a living is on the land. The land is owned by a small number of people: the *landowning class*. The landowners live in wealth and splendour – at the expense of everyone else. Nearly everyone else is forced to work as peasants on the land of the landowning class. They do not have any choice in the matter because they do not have any land of their own and there is no other way to make a living.

As time goes by progress is made and important new ways of making a living develop – through trading, banking, factories ... A powerful new class of traders, bankers and factory owners grows up. They are the *capitalist class*. Soon this new class is so powerful that they overthrow the landowners in a *revolution* and run the country themselves.

Stage 2 Capitalism: The capitalists now run the country in their own interests. They use their money to build up new factories and towns and develop new industries. They turn the country into an *industrial country*. To make a living *now* most people have to go and work for the capitalists as factory workers, miners etc – working for very low wages. Meanwhile the capitalists live in luxury. The *working class* remain very poor, living in terrible conditions.

Marx believed that advanced industrial countries such as Britain, Germany and the USA had reached this stage.

In the end the working class will unite against the capitalists and another *revolution* will take place.

Stage 3 Communism: The workers will rule themselves. Private property will be abolished. Everything will be shared by the community as a whole. Everyone will work for the good of the community. Everyone will be equal.

Marx believed that one day communism would be achieved all over the world. He expected it to happen first in the industrial countries such as Britain and the USA. These countries were already at Stage 2 (capitalism).

Chinese communists believed that the events of 1911 were the beginning of the first revolution which would end feudalism and bring capitalists to power. They saw the Guomindang as the army of the capitalist class.

‘*The gunfire of the Russian Revolution brought Marxism to China.*’ (E)

The Communist Party of China was formed in 1921. It had 57 members. One of them was Mao Zedong, who became First Secretary of the Hunan Province communists. The Chinese communists looked to the USSR for leadership. The Soviet leaders told them to work with the Guomindang. With such a small membership the Chinese communists had little chance of achieving anything on their own. Although in communists' eyes the Guomindang was a 'capitalist' party, for the time being their aims were the same. In 1923 Mao wrote:

‘*The present political problem in China is none other than the problem of national revolution. The historic task of the Chinese people is to overthrow the warlords and their allies the foreign enemies. This revolution is the task of the people as a whole.*’ (F)

Although from 1924–7 the Communist Party worked with the Guomindang, their membership grew quickly. As you saw on pages 12–13 the Communists organised strikes and demonstrations in many Chinese cities. Meanwhile Mao was beginning to see the peasants as the most important force for change in China.

Communists were so successful in helping to organise 'peasant associations' that in 1926 Mao was able to tell a Guomindang meeting:

‘*In a very short time, several hundred million peasants in China's central, southern and northern provinces will rise like a tornado – a force so fast and violent that no power however great will be able to stop it. They will break through the chains that hold them and push forward along the road to freedom!*’ (G)

Mao believed there would be a revolution in the countryside. He reported:

‘*A revolution is . . . an act of violence in which one class overthrows another. A rural (country) revolution is one in which the peasants overthrow the feudal landlord class.*’ (H)

Many Guomindang officers were themselves landlords or the sons of landlords. Like Chiang Kaishek they now saw the communists as a danger.

Much of the Guomindang's money came from capitalist businessmen and traders, especially in Shanghai. They faced losing everything, unless the communists were dealt with.

Chiang wondered how far he could trust his communist allies. If the communists saw the Guomindang as 'capitalist' then one day they would try to destroy it. As Chiang Kaishek saw it, either he must destroy communism, or one day it would destroy him.

D Mao Zedong as a young army officer

??????????????

1 a Why are the capitalists so important during stage 2 of Marx's theory of history?
b Use **A** and **C** to explain what Marxists think a communist society would be like.
c What do you think Marx meant by *'the workers have nothing to lose but their chains'* (**B**)?
d What did Mao mean by **E**?
e Why did the communists make an alliance with the Guomindang?
f How did the communists help the Guomindang?
g What reasons did Chiang have for wanting to crush communism?

2 Why might Mao's report to the Guomindang in **G** and **H** have been ill-advised? Why might some communists have been against working with the Guomindang in the first place?

7 MASSACRE!

F Execution of suspected Communist agents in Shanghai

1927. The Guomindang was split. The 'right-wing', led by Chiang Kaishek, wanted to crush the communists at once. The 'left-wing', led by Wang Jingwei, wanted to continue the alliance. When the Guomindang government was moved to Wuhan early in 1927, Wang and the left went on working with the communists.

Chiang ignored the left. A massacre of communists began in the Spring of 1927. It started in Shanghai. J.B. Powell, a news editor in Shanghai at the time, later wrote:

'For a long time the complete story of the Shanghai war between the right-wing Guomindang and the communists could not be told. This was because the Guomindang did not dare to reveal their methods. While those who were suppressed (put down) did not survive to tell the story.' **(A)**

The Guomindang entered Shanghai in April 1927. Until then the city was in the hands of a warlord, Sun Chuanfang. **B** is taken from letters a student in Shanghai wrote to an American friend. They suggest the killings began even before Chiang's forces reached the city:

'19 February: There is a general strike by the Shanghai General Labour Union. The strikers have no weapons at all. The Guomindang armies are still several hundred miles away. A friend of mine who is connected with the Guomindang Party, says that there is some agreement between the Party and Sun Chuanfang.

18 March: The general strike was called off on 24 February, after hundreds of innocent workmen, students and others were killed without trials or even questioning. The International Settlement (foreigners) didn't do any of the killing, they let (Sun Chuanfang's) police and soldiers do their killing for them. They even let them into the International Settlement just for this purpose.

27 March: The city is quiet, except for the daily murders — usually of factory foremen.' **(B)**

The next letter is written over five weeks later:

'6 May: *You must certainly have heard of Chiang's suppression of the communists.*' (C)

Other witnesses are able to fill in some of the details of what happened during those five weeks. Stirling Fessenden, a US official in the International Settlement, tells us:

'*I went down to a large Chinese house with the French police chief. The entrance hall was lined with stacks of rifles and sub-machine guns. There we met Dou Yuseng, a leading Guomindang figure. We got down to business straight away. Dou said he was willing to move against the Reds (communists), but he demanded two things. First, he wanted the French to supply him with at least 5000 rifles and more than enough bullets. Then turning to me he demanded permission to move his trucks through the International Settlement, something which until then had never been granted to any Chinese force.*' (D)

On 12 April 1927 Chiang ordered his troops to move against the Reds. They were to execute all communists. J.B. Powell wrote:

'*the shooting began and continued without stopping for days . . . The communists could not stand up against the experienced gunmen of Dou Yuseng.*' (E)

No one knows how many so-called communists were killed in Shanghai. Some estimates say 5000, others say 15 000. Many of the victims probably had nothing to do with the communists. Some reports suggest that people could be gunned down simply for wearing red clothes. F shows one such execution taking place.

The fighting quickly spread to other towns and cities. Photograph G was taken in Guangzhou. It shows two 'Reds' who have been executed.

Chiang now declared Nanjing the new capital of China. For a while Wang and the left in Wuhan continued to support the communists. They were forced to give in when Chiang's army marched on Wuhan. Chiang was helped by British and US warships which blocked the Yangtze River, cutting off supplies to Wuhan.

Many years later Mao Zedong wrote:

'*Communist leaders were now ordered by the Party to leave the country and go to Russia, or other places of safety . . . I persuaded the Party to send me back to Hunan instead . . .*

In September we succeeded in organising widespread risings (the Autumn Harvest Risings) through the peasant unions of Hunan. The first units of a peasant-worker army were formed.' (H)

The Guomindang quickly dealt with these risings.

G   Dead 'Reds' in the streets of Guangzhou

They then encouraged landlords to execute any peasants who might be communist supporters. In the next three years thousands of peasants were murdered. (One of those arrested was Mao's young wife Yang Kaihui. In 1930 she was shot.) Meanwhile Mao had led the remains of his peasants' army into the mountains on the Hunan-Jiangxi border. It seemed that the communists were finished.

Chiang's forces continued to move north. The remaining warlords were either defeated or agreed to support the Guomindang. In 1928 Chiang took Beijing. He changed the name of the city to Peiping, meaning 'Northern Peace'. Nanjing was to remain the capital of China. Chiang declared that only one party would be allowed in China while the people were being 'trained for democracy' – that was the Guomindang. China had become a one-party state.

??????????????

1 a Why did the Guomindang split?
b Why were most people not sure what had happened in Shanghai for years after the killings of 1927 (**A**)?
c What evidence is there that the Guomindang did not start the massacre in Shanghai?
d In what ways did foreign countries help Chiang in 1927? *Why* do you think they helped him?
e What were the 'Autumn Harvest Risings' (**H**)?

2 Look at the map on the inside front cover. Why do you think Chiang made Nanjing the capital of China?

3 Look at **G**. What evidence is there in the photograph to suggest that such killings were an everyday event in Guangzhou?

4 As though you are a supporter of the communists, write a series of diary entries describing what happened to you, your friends, your family, the communists, and China during 1927 and 1928.

8 The Red Army

A General Zhu De

Mao Zedong set up a new communist base in the winter of 1927–8. It was high in the Jinggangshan Mountains on the Jiangxi-Hunan border. Mao had less than 1000 men with him. In the spring of 1928 he was joined by another small army of 2000 men under General Zhu De (A). Zhu was an ex-warlord who had become a communist. During 1928 more and more peasants came to the Jinggangshan stronghold. Soon the numbers had risen to over 12 000 men. This force became known as the *Red Army*.

Soon the Red Army was under attack from the Guomindang. Mao wrote a Report to the Central Committee of the Chinese Communist Party (in Shanghai and Russia) in 1928:

The average soldier needs six months or a year's training before he can fight. Our soldiers, recruited only yesterday, have to fight today with almost no training to speak of. They fight by courage alone . . . (B)

Sections of the Red Army often found themselves fighting with hardly any weapons at all. A Chinese–American historian called Han Suyin visited Jinggangshan in the 1960s. A peasant told her about one attack on the Red Army in August 1928:

We made bamboo spikes, 100 for each person. Everyone helped. We sowed these spikes on all the pathways leading into the mountain. Then came the enemy troops, many of them, and for two days they surrounded the mountain. On the third day they were going to attack. At first there had been mist in the valleys. When it lifted we saw the enemy, but they did not see us for it was Summer, thick with the trees and bushes on the mountain slopes. (C)

He went on to explain how the Red Army were able to fight off the Guomindang attack, although they were desperately short of arms and ammunition. Their tactics were designed to use the rough countryside to their own advantage.

The enemy troops opened fire by shelling the slopes of the mountain pass. We did not fire back for we had so few guns. But our soldiers crept under the bushes, nearer and nearer, while the enemy fire went over our heads. Three or four times their fire raked the slopes and then stopped, and we knew they were about to advance. Then our one and only mortar (a gun which fires small shells) was made to shoot. It had only three shells, so only one was fired. This shell fell right among some soldiers and wounded or killed no more than six. But it was so unexpected that the enemy were really confused. Until then we had kept completely silent, not even moving a stone. Now, all at once we made such a racket with gongs, drums and firecrackers while also shouting and screaming, and because we were so near them – much nearer than they had thought – they ran away! (D)

Mao and Zhu saw that the Red Army would have to be very cunning to have a chance against armies ten times their size. They had to avoid all-out battles at any cost. Mao summed up their new guerilla tactics with these words:

*The enemy advances, we retreat.
The enemy camps, we harass.
The enemy tires, we attack.
The enemy retreats, we pursue.* (E)

Mao claimed the Red Army was organised on very different lines to other armies. He wrote in his report:

❛*The officers do not beat the men. Officers and men receive equal treatment. Soldiers can meet as they like and they can speak freely. Glossy badges and ceremonies have been got rid of. The account books are open for all to look at.*

The newly captured soldiers in particular feel that our army and the Guomindang's army are worlds apart. Although they hardly get any money in the Red Army, they feel they are now free. The fact that the same soldier who was not brave in the enemy army yesterday becomes very brave in the Red Army today shows how democracy affects them. The Red Army is like a furnace in which all captured soldiers are melted down and completely changed . . .❜ (F)

Nevertheless in 1930, when a section of the Red Army revolted, over 2000 soldiers were shot on Mao's orders.

The historian Han Suyin, a life-long supporter of Mao Zedong, tells us:

❛*Mao Zedong began giving regular lectures, without tiring, almost every afternoon. These became models for those discussion meetings which took place at every level in China after 1949. Ignorant western writers have said this was just 'brainwashing'. In reality these meetings were the beginnings of educating people about democracy.*❜ (G)

In private Mao does not seem to have been confident about the future. In November 1928 he noted:

❛*Wherever the Red Army goes, the people are cold and keep their distance. Only after propaganda* (teaching about communism) *do they slowly move into action. Whatever enemy units we face there are hardly any cases of soldiers deserting to join our side. We have to fight it out . . . We feel we are isolated and keep hoping this isolation will end.*❜ (H)

Mao and Zhu knew that the Red Army could only be successful if it had the support of the peasants. They drew up Six Principles of the Red Army:

❛*1 Put back all doors when you leave a house* (doors are wooden boards also used as beds).
2 Rice-stalk mattresses must all be bundled up again and returned.
3 Be polite. Help people when you can.
4 Give back everything you borrow, even if it's only a needle.
5 Pay for all things broken, even if only a chopstick.
6 Don't help yourself or search for things when people are not in their houses.❜ (J)

K Red Army soldiers going into action, armed with spears and swords

The Red Army continued to grow, and it captured more weapons from the Guomindang. In November 1928 Mao was joined by Peng Dehuai. The two were to work together for the next 30 years. Peng brought another communist army. But there was not enough food to go round. The Red Army had to break out from its base. In January 1929 Zhu and Mao led the Red Army south-east to Southern Jiangxi. **K** shows a section of the Red Army on the move. Nearly half the men died on the way. Some were killed in battle, others died of cold and hunger.

With the support of the peasants, it did not take the Red Army long to take control of Southern Jiangxi. They then took the land away from the landlords and gave it to the peasants. 'Collective farming' was started: this meant that the peasants had to share the land between them and work on it together.

The lives of women also changed. In 1930 Hu Yepin, a communist still living in Shanghai, wrote a story called *Living Together*. It is based on what he had heard about life in Southern Jiangxi:

Conditions now have changed a lot. Men who once lived in poverty have become lively and merry. Women's lives have changed even more. They used to live shut up in poor homes going through the endless rounds of cooking, washing, caring for the children, feeding the pigs — shut up like prisoners in a jail without hope for the future. Now they are like birds soaring in the sky. Their life has become free. They are no longer put down, nor do they fear their husbands. They can have relationships with men as they choose. There is even public help in looking after the children . . . (**L**)

However the Communist Party was now split. The Party leaders were worried by Mao and the Red Army. They doubted whether Mao was a true Marxist. Stalin, the ruler of the USSR, shared the views of Mao's enemies. Marx had said that the *workers* in the towns and cities must lead the communist revolution (communism is meant to be about workers taking over). The Red Army was a *peasants'* army. Mao seemed to be expecting peasants to bring about the communist revolution. Mao wrote to the Central Committee in 1929:

It is a mistake to fear the growing power of the peasants. The revolution will not fail simply because the peasants become more powerful than the workers. (**M**)

In 1931 the area under Red Army control was declared 'The Chinese Soviet Republic'. Mao was its Chairman. There were now over a million people living under communist rule in China.

??????????????

1 a Where did Mao Zedong set up his new base?
b Who was Zhu De?
c Where were most members of the Central Committee of the Chinese Communist Party?
d Where did the Red Army move to in 1929? Why?

2 What do you think was the aim of Mao's Six Principles for the Red Army (**J**)? Are there any more principles that you think could be added?

3 How far can you trust the evidence on these pages? Draw a chart like the one below and fill it in. For each piece of evidence *think*:
a Is the writer/photographer trying to mislead?
b Are they themselves being misled?
c Are they in a position to know the truth?

Source	Type of evidence	What it tells us	Reasons for trusting/not trusting it
B	primary Communist Party report	1928 Red Army had no training but were very brave.	Can probably be trusted. Mao's account is supported by the peasant's account (**C**). Mao has no reason to lie – except that if the Red Army is beaten people will be less likely to blame him, and if it one day defeats the enemy Mao can take extra credit.
C/D			
E			
F			
G			
J			
K			

4 Imagine you are an old peasant who fought with Mao in the Red Army. You have been asked to tell a group of foreign tourists about your experiences. Describe: joining the Red Army; your leader, Mao Zedong; living in the mountains; life in the Army; fighting; moving to Southern Jianxi.

9 The Nationalist Government

A How the Japanese conquered Manchuria

On 18 September 1931, 50 000 Japanese soldiers invaded Manchuria. **A** is a German cartoon showing how they conquered the area. Thousands of people were killed. The League of Nations protested against the invasion but did nothing to make the Japanese pull out. Manchuria was an important industrial area. There were also 800 000 Japanese people living in the region (along with 30 million Chinese and two million Manchus). Japan was by far the strongest country in the Far East.

Most Chinese people expected Chiang Kaishek to do something. Demonstrations were held in Nanjing, Beijing and other big cities, demanding that Chiang should stand up to the Japanese.

The invasion of Manchuria was just one of the problems Chiang's Nationalist Government faced. There were many others:

Warlords Chiang's government was still not in full control of the whole of China. Many of the warlords who

21

had surrendered or made peace with the Guomindang during the Northern Expedition still had powerful armies. In 1931 there were over two million soldiers in China. Sichuan and Inner Mongolia still had powerful warlords. The most remote parts of the old Chinese empire, Tibet, Xinjiang and Outer Mongolia had really become independent countries.

Poverty During the time of the warlords and the Northern Expedition it was the peasants who suffered the most. In many parts of China peasants had their crops destroyed or stolen by the fighting armies. Xu Zhimo, a poet, wrote to a friend in England in 1929:

‘Whole provinces are dragging on in terrible conditions. I myself have seen the starvation in the north, and my blood turns cold with the thought of it. Children that no longer look human fight over mosses that their bony fingers scratch off cracks in rocks and stuff into their mouths, in their efforts to ease their hunger and cold. Lord, why did you let these children be born!’ (B)

A British diplomat, Malcolm MacDonald, who was in China in 1929 later wrote:

‘Throughout the vast rural areas nearly all the peasants continued to be poverty-stricken. They were often so half-starved that in order to be able to buy enough food to keep themselves alive, parents had to sell their children to their landlords or to businessmen. Frequently husbands were, for the same reasons, forced to sell their wives.’ (C)

MacDonald came across a young prostitute in Beijing. He managed to talk to her about her past:

‘I learnt that she was still a youngster in her middle teens. Her parents had been poor peasants. Her happiest memories concerned her infant years with her parents, despite the fact that they were so poor. Alas! She had not seen or heard of them for many years, and did not even know whether they were still alive. She had been sold twice – first as a child by her helpless father to their landlord, and later by that 'gentleman' to a brothel.’ (D)

Many of the Guomindang officers were themselves landlords. Chiang could not afford to upset them.

The economy China had been lent a lot of money by foreign governments and banks. Every year the Chinese government had to pay out large amounts just to pay the interest on these debts. For instance the Belgian *Societe-Générale* had lent the government the money to build China's few railways. By 1931 China's railway debt alone was 1300 million US dollars. Chiang's government was still getting money from western businessmen (especially in Shanghai). But this would only go on as long as Chiang continued to put down communists. There was still very little modern industry in China. The industry that did exist was either in Manchuria or owned by foreign companies.

Opposition The Red Army in Jiangxi was getting stronger. Chiang had three 'Extermination Campaigns'

DECISION MAKER

In groups one member of your group is Chiang Kaishek. The rest of you are members of his Nanjing government. You agree about these aims: to stay in power; to keep Nanjing in control of as much of China as possible; to crush communism; to make China more modern.

Bearing these aims in mind how will you deal with the problems facing you?

Here are some of the things your government could do:

1 Declare war on Japan.
2 Hold a meeting with Mao and other communist leaders. See if a new alliance can be started to defeat the Japanese in Manchuria.
3 Protest to the Japanese government about the invasion of Manchuria. Encourage the people to demonstrate against the Japanese.
4 Avoid upsetting the Japanese in case they take further action. Use the police to break up anti-Japanese demonstrations.
5 March against the warlords in Sichuan and Inner Mongolia. Try to reconquer Tibet and Xinjiang.
6 Leave the warlords alone where possible. Only fight against them as a last resort.
7 Take the land away from the landlords (as the Red Army is doing). Divide it up among the peasants.
8 Get each region to do what it can to help the peasants in the worst-affected areas, by setting up soup kitchens (but nothing too expensive).
9 Borrow more money to help feed the people in the poorest areas.
10 Make landowners pay more taxes. End the taxes paid by the poorest peasants.
11 Borrow more money to build new railways, factories, schools and universities to make China more modern.
12 *Nationalise* (bring into government ownership) the banks and other important companies. Nationalise all foreign businesses.
13 Increase taxes to pay off China's debts (this will take many years).
14 Start a new 'Extermination Campaign' to smash the Red Army (this will cost a great deal of money).

E Nationalist soldiers preparing to go into action. Why might it be difficult for them to move quickly?

against the Red Army between December 1930 and July 1931. All three failed. In Fujian and Guangzhou the 'Left' Guomindang was still strong. There had also been anti-Japanese riots in parts of the country.

You can find out the policies that Chiang's government actually carried out, inside the back cover.

E shows Guomindang soldiers setting off on an extermination raid against the communists. Malcolm MacDonald tells us:

We held talks with the Guomindang about changing some of the things in the 'Unequal Treaties'. My father happened to be Great Britain's Prime Minister then, so I was made very welcome in Nanjing and elsewhere. Chiang Kaishek himself was off fighting the communists, but I met his charming wife, who obviously had a great deal of influence. I also met the Finance Minister and other government officials. Chiang and his colleagues showed no interest in introducing social and economic reforms which would have helped the masses. (F)

Manchuria became a new country, but it was really controlled by the Japanese. They made ex-Emperor Puyi its ruler. In January 1932 the Japanese attacked Shanghai. There had been anti-Japanese riots in the city. Against Chiang's orders, the Nineteenth Route Army of the Guomindang started to fight back. They fought so fiercely that in the end the Japanese were forced to withdraw from Shanghai. In May 1932 there was a ceasefire. Chiang moved the Nineteenth Route Army south to Fujian where he thought they would be out of the way.

The problems facing Chiang's Nationalist Government were always too great for them to solve – if they aimed to wipe out communism at the same time.

---

15 Use your growing secret police force to seek out and arrest all suspected communists.
16 Use the secret police to arrest suspected opponents of the government, whether they are communists or not.
17 Hold government elections, like those in Britain and USA. Allow anyone to be a candidate, and everyone over 18 to vote.
18 Hold elections – but ban communists from taking part.
19 Anything else.

a Choose the policies you think the government should follow if it is going to meet its aims. If you cannot agree then it is up to Chiang to make the final decisions.
b In real life you probably disagree with some or all of the aims of Chiang's government. Look at the list again. Which of the policies would *you* really like to see carried out by the government? Try to persuade the rest of the group round to your point of view. What would happen if those policies were actually put into action?

10 The Long March

What is the longest distance you have ever walked in a day? Think how tired you felt at the end of it. Think how tired you would feel if you had to repeat that walk every day for a year. These pages look at one of the longest walks in history. It began in 1934.

In 1932 the Jiangxi Soviet had declared war on Japan, although the nearest Japanese soldiers were thousands of miles away. To many Chinese people this showed that the communists were ready to fight against the invaders while all Chiang did was give in to them. Meanwhile Mao defeated Chiang's Fourth Extermination Campaign.

Early in 1933 the Chinese Communist Party finally moved its headquarters from Shanghai to the Jiangxi Soviet. Some of the Shanghai Communist leaders did not agree with Mao's brand of communism (see pages 14–15). For the next two years Mao was allowed little say in Party affairs.

By 1933 it was beginning to look as though the Communist Party would not last much longer. The Guomindang had new army advisers and new plans. The new advisers were German. They included General Hans Von Seeckt. He would not allow Guomindang forces to follow the communists deep into Red Army territory where they could easily be ambushed. Instead he completely surrounded the Jiangxi Soviet, using over 700 000 men. A network of forts, trenches and barbed wire was built around the Red Army base and patrolled by armoured cars, tanks and aircraft. These fortifications were the base for attacks on the Red Army.

The communists now found that their supplies were cut off. It looked as if this Fifth Extermination Campaign would be a success: the Red Army would finally be smashed. Mao later wrote:

The Red Armies milled around between the enemy's main forces and his forts and were unable to do anything. This was really the worst and most stupid way to fight. (A)

The Guomindang used the same methods against smaller communist bases elsewhere in China (map B).

Then in 1933 the Guomindang Nineteenth Route Army based at Fujian revolted. These were the same soldiers who had fought against the Japanese at Shanghai. They were angry at the way Chiang kept giving in to the Japanese instead of fighting them. They offered to make an alliance with the communists. Chiang set off towards Fujian to crush the rebels.

Meanwhile Von Seeckt's methods were gradually destroying the Red Army. During the next year communist leaders had to take some important decisions.

So what *should* the Red Army leaders do?

In 1933 and 1934 there were a number of choices open to them. Here are some of them. *In groups:* look at each of them in turn. Work out what *you* think the Red Army should do. Choose one or more of the plans, or work out one of your own.

1 Alliance with the Fujian rebels
Find Fujian on map **B**. An alliance with the rebels would defeat Chiang's attempts to surround the Jiangxi Soviet. Fujian has a long coast and ports: weapons, ammunition and food could be brought in to supply the Red Army. Fighting together, the Fujian rebels and the Red Army might have a chance against the Guomindang, although you would still be greatly outnumbered.

2 Break out to Sichuan
Try to break through the Guomindang fortifications at their weakest point in the west. This alone is likely to cost thousands of men. Then march west as quickly as possible into some of the most remote provinces in China. Set up a new base in Sichuan and try to rebuild the Red Army. The whole of the Red Army will have to walk. This will mean crossing wide rivers such as the Yangtze and Tatu. (The Red Army does not have any boats. All bridges will be strongly guarded or destroyed before the Red Army arrives). The men will have to cross some of the highest mountains in China, with little gear to protect them against the cold. The Guomindang will be able to attack you for most of the way. You will face air attacks, shelling, ambushes and have to fight many battles. Chiang is not fully in control of Sichuan. In effect it is still ruled by warlords. They are unlikely to want a Red Army base in Sichuan.

3 Break out to North Shaanxi
Break through the Guomindang barrier to the west as in No. 2. As soon as you can, turn north towards Shaanxi. In north Shaanxi there is another communist force. If you make it that far you will be able to join up with the north Shaanxi communists. You will still have to face all the problems mentioned in No. 2 *and* you will have to march thousands of miles further. Once in the north you will be better placed to fight the Japanese.

4 Split up
Divide the Red Army into four or more groups of about 20 000 men each. Try to break out in different directions,

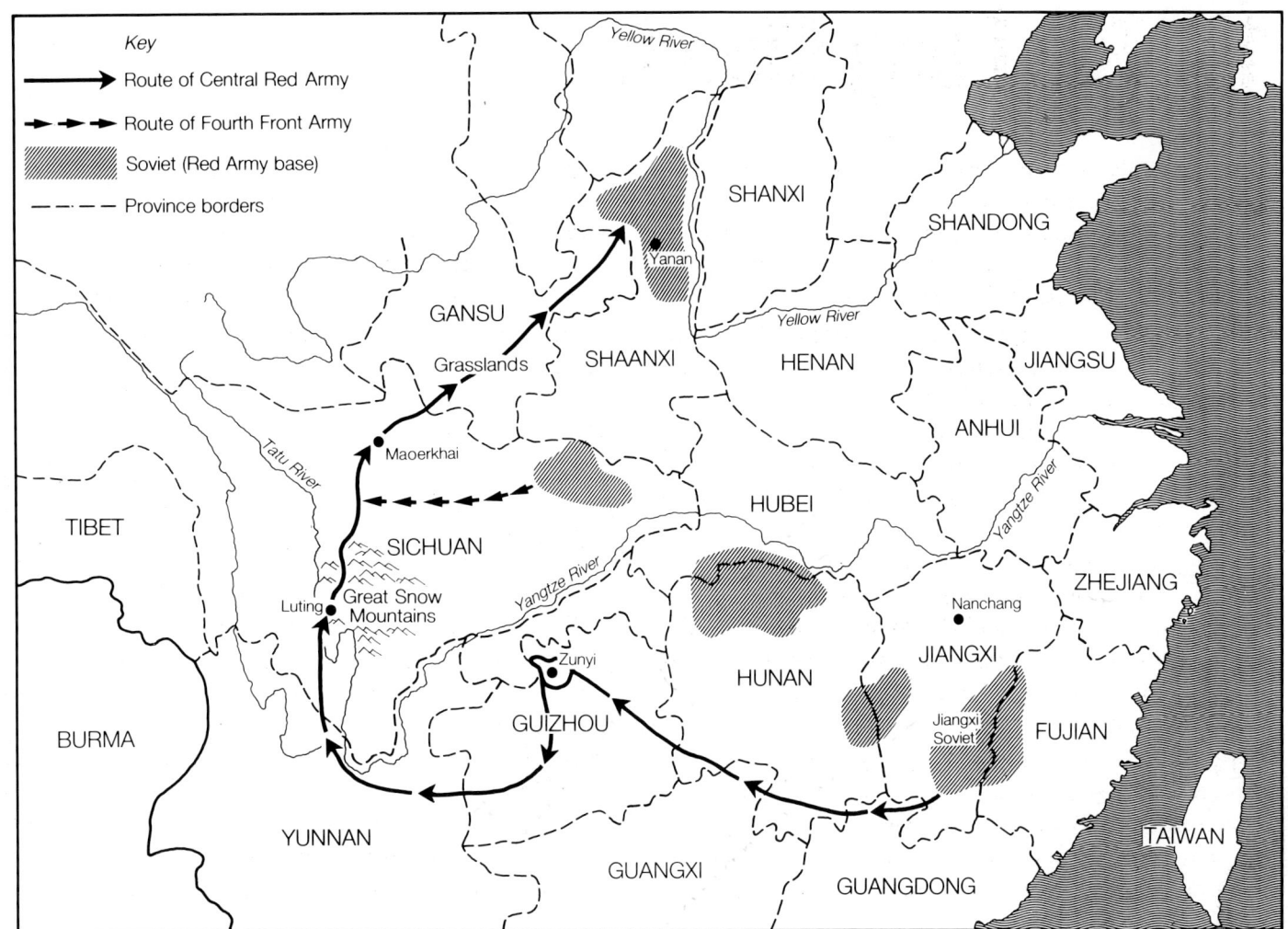

B   The route of the Long March

each group heading for north or west China. This may confuse the enemy and perhaps one of the groups will survive to set up a new communist base in a remote part of China.

5   Forward Offensive Policy
Attack is the best form of defence! Use part of the Red Army to break out to the north, while Chiang is putting down the Fujian Rebels. Attack Nanchang and other cities in the area. Chiang's fortifications will have to be broken up in order to follow. The policy of all-out attack worked against the Fourth Extermination Campaign. As Zhou Enlai says 'Hit the enemy beyond the gate.' The Guomindang forces are now much stronger than they were during the Fourth Extermination Campaign. The Red Army is much weaker.

6   Hold talks with Chiang
Try to start ceasefire talks with Chiang. Try to get him to see that the real enemy of China is Japan. The communists and Guomindang had worked together for most of the Northern Expedition against the warlords. Perhaps Chiang will see reason after all.

The Long March Begins

The Red Army leaders refused to make an alliance with the Fujian rebels. They announced:

'The Fujian People's Revolutionary Government is no different from the rest of the Guomindang. Its activities are nothing more than a decoy to hoodwink the people.' (C)

Chiang was able to crush them without interference from the Red Army. The ring of fortifications around the Jiangxi Soviet was made stronger.

On the night of 15–16 October 1934 the Central Red Army attacked the Guomindang fortifications at their weakest point, in the west. After heavy fighting 100 000 men managed to break out. Other Red Army groups –

E An artist's view of Mao Zedong leading the Long March

the Second Front Army and the Fourth Front Army – also broke out from communist bases in the north and headed west. The Long March had begun.

Each man carried his own baggage. Mules were used to carry weapons, ammunition, money, food, gold and even printing presses. A Red Army soldier remembers:

Well, we ourselves did not know at the beginning that we were actually on the Long March and that it was going to be such a big thing. All we knew was that we were getting out of the bases. We were surrounded and being choked, a million men against us – tanks, aeroplanes . . . We broke through one ring of fortifications, then a second, then a third, and we marched westward always westward. We had the rain soaking us to the skin and the wind in our faces. We headed towards Sichuan province, for Sichuan was not letting Chiang Kaishek come in . . .

But we had so much equipment with us – tons of stores and even bedding and furniture, all sorts of things. This slowed us down. We were about 100 000 in number and could easily be seen, a long slow caravan of men and mules. Every day we were attacked by the Guomindang and sometimes by warlords.
(D)

E is a Chinese painting showing the Red Army on the Long March. In January 1935 the Central Red Army reached Zunyi. This city was held by Guomindang forces. The communists managed to capture it almost without bloodshed. Red Army soldiers dressed up in stolen Guomindang uniforms and walked into the city. The Guomindang did not realise what was happening until it was too late. Even so, things looked bad for the Red Army. In three months over half the men who had broken out from the Jiangxi base had been killed. It seemed to be only a question of time before the rest of the Red Army was destroyed. The same soldier tells us:

When we got to Zunyi we held a big conference to study our position. By that time most of us wanted Mao Zedong to lead us and no one else. When we listened to him we were successful; when we did not we were defeated. So a great clamour went through the Red Army: 'Listen to Comrade Mao Zedong!'.

. . . The first thing that Comrade Mao made us do was to throw away all the useless things we carried with us.
(F)

Mao was now in effect Chairman of the Chinese Communist Party. As the Red Army continued to be attacked Mao was forced to move deeper into western Sichuan. Sometimes they marched 40 miles in a day. With each day that passed more men were lost. Some were killed by the enemy, others died of exposure. The sick and wounded had to be left behind with friendly peasants. Unlike the Guomindang the Red Army won support in the areas it marched through. The Communists bought their food from the peasants, they did not steal it.

On 30 May 1935 the Red Army crossed the Tatu River after a crack unit stormed the Luting Bridge. Then they had to go over the Great Snow Mountains. Another Red Army soldier remembers:

'Heavy fog was all around us. There was a high wind and it began to rain. As we climbed higher there was a terrible hail storm. The air became so thin we could hardly breathe. It was impossible to speak. The cold was so dreadful that our breath froze and our hands and lips turned blue. Men and animals staggered and fell into chasms, disappearing forever. Those who sat down to rest or go to the toilet froze to death on the spot.' (G)

Having crossed these mountains Mao's Red Army managed to join up with the Fourth Front Army led by Zhang Guodao.

Zhang and Mao could not agree on what to do now. Zhang wanted to retreat into Sichuan and start a new Soviet there. Mao wanted to head north-east towards North Shaanxi where there was already a communist base. In North Shaanxi, Mao believed, the Red Army would be able to re-build and would be better placed to fight against the Japanese. People would come to see the Communist Party as the only patriotic party in China.

However, to get to North Shaanxi the Red Army would have to make the dangerous crossing over the Grasslands of Qinghai. This was a barren area of swamp and quicksand, with no roads across it, and little to eat. After much argument, Mao had his way and the Red Army moved onto the Grasslands. This was the most terrible part of the whole Long March. The swamps were so deadly that if a man took one wrong step he could disappear completely. One soldier said:

'Men had to sleep standing in pairs or groups of four, back to back – or else drown in the mud.' (H)

The mud was not only foul and strinking, it was also poisonous. Soldiers' legs swelled up so much that they could hardly walk. Mosquito bites turned their faces black. It rained all the time. After the men had eaten their mules and horses they ran out of food. They tried eating wild plants, but most of these were poisonous, causing diarrhoea, sickness and sometimes death. In the end they boiled and ate their boots and belts.

In October 1935 the remains of Mao's Red Army arrived in Northern Shaanxi. The soldier who provided D and F continues:

'So we survived the long journey. 100 000 of us had left the base in October 1934. Less than 20 000 (probably nearer 10 000) reached Yanan in October 1935. We were not disheartened. And we trusted Mao Zedong. So we began all over again' (J)

In 1936 the survivors were joined by the Second Front Army. By the end of the year the Red Army's strength was back to 80 000 men. Yanan was to remain the communist headquarters until 1947.

Here are some of the things that have been said about the Long March.

'It was a great nationalist victory.' (K)
Chiang Kaishek

'The story of the Long March needs its own volumes. In the history of mankind it will stand forever a monument to man's courage, endurance and daring.' (L)
Han Suyin (writer)

'In fact . . . the Long March was a great retreat. Only about one-tenth of those who started out survived it. And after it the communists were still on the point of being completely destroyed.' (M)
James Pinckney Harrison (historian)

'We swept across a distance of more than 6500 miles on our own two feet, across 11 provinces . . . The Long March is a manifesto. It declares to the world that the Red Army is an army of heroes and that . . . Chiang Kaishek and the like are as nothing. It shows Chiang's complete failure. The Long March also tells the 200 million people in 11 provinces that only the road of the Red Army leads to their liberation . . . It has sown many seeds in 11 provinces, which will bear fruit and yield a crop in the future. To sum up, the Long March has ended in our victory and the enemy's deafeat.' (N)
Mao Zedong

Whether it was a victory or a defeat, the Long March probably changed the course of history.

??????????????

1 **a** Who was Hans Von Seekt?
   b Why did the 19th Route Army in Fujian revolt?
   c Why was the Zunyi Conference so important?
   d What did Mao mean in **N** when he said the Long March had 'sown many seeds'?

2 **a** Look at **E**. What do you think the artist is saying about the Long March?
   b What details in **E** are most likely to be wrong?
   c How far can we trust **F** and **J** as sources of evidence?

3 Which of comments **K** to **N** do you think best sums up the Long March? Why?

11 China Invaded

In December 1936 Chiang Kaishek was kidnapped. He had tried to start a Sixth Extermination Campaign against the Shaanxi communist base. Some of the Guomindang troops who were meant to fight in this campaign were from Manchuria. They did not want to fight the communists, they wanted to fight the Japanese. Instead of obeying Chiang's orders they kidnapped him from his headquarters at Xian. They only let him go after he had met Zhou Enlai (a leading communist) and agreed to form a United Front against the Japanese.

For the next three years the communists and the Guomindang stopped fighting each other. Officially the Red Army became the Eighth Route Army of the Guomindang. This alliance was made just in time. On 7 July 1937 Japanese soldiers attacked Chinese troops at the Marco Polo Bridge, north of Beijing. The Japanese invasion of the rest of China had begun. They planned to build an empire for themselves.

Japanese armies quickly overran most of northern China. The fighting was bitter and bloody. Neither side believed in taking prisoners. In August Shanghai was captured after heavy fighting. In December 1937 Nanjing fell. Thousands of civilians there were murdered by Japanese soldiers. Many of the women were raped before being shot or stabbed. During 1938 one major city after another fell to the Japanese. Millions of people fled from the invaders. Han Suyin, then a nurse in China, describes what she saw:

I went to the ward and saw two girl soldiers; one of them had her leg torn to shreds . . . I wonder what happened to them . . . the Japanese bayoneted wounded soldiers whenever they found them. They had done so in Nanjing, killing all the wounded and all the Chinese nurses and doctors too . . . (In Changsha) whole families exhausted with walking lay with their bundles in the clogged streets or by the riverside, mopping their faces. They lined the roads and riverbanks as far as one

B Chinese peasants escaping from the Japanese

C Survivors in the wreckage of a Shanghai railway station

could see. Most went in the same general direction. Others stopped and waited where they were because they lay dying or were simply too tired to go on. There were millions taking to the roads, going out of the city, spreading into the countryside, westward. And the Japanese planes strafed (machine-gunned) them . . .

The roads were ploughed mud and dirt. Carts dragged by men, the ropes biting into their shoulders, went by; trucks piled high with bedding and furniture, buses loaded so heavy that they overturned, and people plodding on, carrying their children . . . (A)

B shows refugees fleeing from the Japanese. C shows the effects of Japanese bombing.

As they retreated Chiang ordered his armies to *scorch the earth*, to destroy anything that could be of use to the enemy. Han Suyin tells us:

On 12 November 1938 the city of Changsha was in great part destroyed by fire, not started by the Japanese but by the Guomindang themselves. In their stupid scorched earth policies they laid waste all about them. This was more harmful to their own people than the enemy. In the spring the Yellow River dykes had been breached by order of Chiang Kaishek to flood the land and stop the Japanese. It had not stopped them, though it did flood the land, and a million Chinese peasants were drowned. (D)

Chiang's armies retreated into Sichuan. The Japanese airforce continued to fight against the Nationalists.

The bombing by the Japanese which began in 1939 continued in 1941 and 1942, with increasing fierceness. Being bombed was part of normal everyday life.

We went to the dug-out when the first alert of the day sounded and there we spent the day. Many people died, both in the bombings and also in the air raid shelters – especially babies – from heat exhaustion and diarrhoea. After 1940 it became dangerous to wipe the sweat off our faces with a handkerchief. There was a rumour that 'spies' had been caught signalling to the planes with white handkerchiefs. Anyone 'signalling' was to be executed at once. One day I saw a man with his hands tied up, with his face covered with a black cloth, being marched off by three soldiers. Behind them came a man in plain clothes holding a revolver. The prisoner would probably be shot through the back of the neck. This method was also used by the secret police for getting rid of 'communists' . . . (E)

It was difficult for the Japanese army to attack Chiang's forces in Sichuan. It was just as difficult for the Nationalist forces to attack the Japanese. The Japanese turned their efforts to smashing the communist forces in Shaanxi.

Between 1936 and 1939 the Red Army had been rebuilt. Even though they were very short of weapons they put up a stiff resistance to the invaders. A Red Army song describes how they fought the Japanese:

'*We are all experts with the gun,
Every bullet gets a foe,
We are the army with wings,
Unafraid of high mountains or deep water.*

*In the thick forest, everywhere
Are the shelters of our comrades,
On the highest ridges and summits,
Are our numberless brothers.*

*Nothing to eat, nothing to wear,
But the enemy gives us food and clothes.
No guns in our hands, no bullets,
The enemy makes them for us to use.*

*We are the people who were born here,
And every inch of ground is ours.
If anyone wants to invade it,
We shall fight him to the death.*' (F)

The Red Army had a brilliant new general called Lin Biao. He would one day become one of the most powerful men in China. In 1940 he helped plan 'The Hundred Regiments Offensive'. Japanese troops in five provinces were attacked by 400 000 Red Army soldiers. The soldiers cut off Japanese units by destroying railways, roads and canals and cutting telegraph wires. Ordinary peasants also helped in this work. Once the Japanese units were cut off they could be dealt with one by one by the Red Army. The Red Army did not believe in taking prisoners either.

The Japanese took revenge with the 'Three-Alls Campaign' (1941–2): '*Kill all, loot all, burn all*'. They did not try to fight the Red Army. Instead they destroyed villages and crops, murdering thousands of peasants. No one knows how many died. Some of the junior Japanese officers had been against this campaign. They knew what would happen: the peasants now hated the invaders even more, and gave even more help to the Red Army. Mao wrote:

'*When we see the enemy, we must not be frightened to death like a rat who sees a cat, simply because he has a weapon in his hands. We must not be afraid of getting close to him or creeping into his midst in order to carry out sabotage. Why should we fear the fact that he has weapons? We can find a way to seize his weapons. All we are afraid of is getting killed by the enemy. But when we have to put up with the suffering the enemy puts us through, how can anyone still fear death? So when we see the enemy, we must act as though they are bread, which can satisfy our hunger, and swallow them.*' (G)

Support for the communists grew.

The Japanese were hated in all the areas of China they occupied. In the towns they often treated the workers like slaves. An old miner in Datong remembered how ordinary people were made to suffer by the Japanese:

'*Our whole family fled from famine in 1939. We came here begging for food. We were captured and forced down the mines. We worked 13 to 16 hours a day. They whipped us every day. The Japanese did not treat the workers like human beings, but like animals. 'Exchange coal with Chinese people's lives,' was their slogan. They used to say, 'There are so many Chinese. Killing them is like killing chickens. When you kill one there are always more.'*

The workers had to drink the stinking water at the bottom of the coal pit. When people became seriously ill they tied their legs and arms, carried them away and kicked them into this hole. Dogs were waiting down there, biting and tearing the bodies to pieces . . . I was then 9 years old, and I was sent to work in the coal pit. I was always beaten by the Japanese, because I was a child and I couldn't do any heavy work.' (H)

The Japanese secret police arrested anyone they thought might cause trouble. These people were sometimes tortured, sometimes shot, and often simply disappeared forever.

Meanwhile the alliance between the Nationalists and the Communists had ended. In January 1941 fighting broke out between Nationalist forces and the Communist New Fourth Army. Chiang Kaishek was worried at the speed with which the communist forces were developing. He turned against them. Within a few days part of the New Fourth Army had been wiped out.

China could no longer be called one country: the south and west was Nationalist China, the north-west was Communist China and the rest was Occupied China. There were now three Chinas.

??????????????

1 a Why was Chiang Kaishek kidnapped in 1936? What did he have to agree to do?
b What probably happened to the two girl soldiers Han Suyin mentions in **A**?
c What was the *scorched earth policy*? What does it tell us about Chiang Kaishek?
d What was the 'Three–Alls Campaign'? Why were junior Japanese officers against it?

2 a In what ways does Han Suyin try to gain the sympathy of the reader (or support for her views) in **A**, **D** and **E**?
b Are **A**, **D** and **E** primary or secondary sources?

3 What does the Red Army song **F** tell us about the way they fought?

12 Communist Victory

'The Japanese are a disease of the skin, the communists are a disease of the heart.' (A)

Chiang Kaishek, 1941

In 1941, the communists were once again fighting the Guomindang, as well as the Japanese. Mao later wrote:

'The time of greatest hardship was in 1940 and 1941 when the Guomindang made two big attacks on the communists. For a while we almost reached a point where we had no clothes to wear, no oil to cook with, no paper, no vegetables, no footwear for the soldiers, and in winter no bedding for the people.' (B)

Yet within eight years Mao's forces were in control of nearly all of China. The evidence on these pages shows how this happened.

Defeating Japan

On 7 December 1941 Japanese planes attacked the US naval base at Pearl Harbor. They also invaded Burma and Malaya and attacked Hong Kong. (See map on inside front cover.) Japan was now at war with the USA and Britain. The fighting in China became part of the Second World War.

Japan was building up an empire in the Far East. On Christmas Day, Hong Kong surrendered. On 15 February 1942 the British base at Singapore fell, after the Japanese had conquered Malaya. The British were forced to retreat from Burma into India, as the Japanese advanced.

The British had been using the 'Burma Road' to get supplies to Chiang Kaishek's armies. This was now cut off. For the next three years the British and Americans airlifted supplies to Chiang Kaishek. Chiang also got some aid from the USSR, which angered Chinese communists. However, Chiang did not use these supplies to attack the Japanese. He simply waited. He was sure that Japan would one day be beaten, now that the USA was in the war.

Most of the fighting in China was between the Japanese and the communists. The Red Army organised the peasants to help in the fight against the Japanese. This was called the 'Mass Line'. C and D tell us how it was done. A Communist Party Central Committee Directive said:

'Party members should go among the masses and lead the people in the fight for their own well-being. They should organise the people into unions, peasant associations, women's leagues, youth corps, children's leagues and self-defence armies to fight against the Japanese and improve the living conditions.' (C)

D was written by an official Chinese communist historian:

'The aim was to get deep behind enemy lines as he advanced. The communists' work teams were organised on the 'three in one' principle: they were to fight as troops, act on behalf of the Party but act like the common people in ordinary times. The armed work teams would appear or disappear unexpectedly in the very heart of the enemy-held areas. The people always knew where they were, but the enemy could never find them. So apart from the huge communist bases there were also many small anti-Japanese positions behind the enemy lines.' (D)

While the peasants helped the Red Army they were also taught about Marxism. Communist bases spread across the whole of northern China. Then in August 1945 US planes dropped atom bombs on the Japanese cities of Hiroshima and Nagasaki. Japan surrendered. Suddenly the war was over. Both Chiang and Mao were taken completely by surprise.

Japan still occupied two-thirds of China. The Americans agreed that Chiang's forces should take the surrender of Japanese garrisons in China, even though many of these were already surrounded by communist troops. US planes flew Nationalist soldiers to the garrisons. Chiang told Japanese soldiers to go on fighting the communists until his men arrived. This meant that Japanese stores of weapons would fall into Nationalist hands.

Russia invades Manchuria

The Russians were also caught by surprise by the sudden ending of the Second World War. In the last six days they had joined the war against Japan by invading Manchuria. Lobsang Thondip, a Manchurian who had been in the Japanese airforce and was in Manchuria at the end of the war, suggests why they invaded:

'The Russians seem to have had a very clear plan of action. They knew exactly where all the industrial areas were, and had detailed plans for the removal of whole industrial plants with their machinery. To carry out their looting they needed all the skilled workers and experts they could lay their hands on. Anshan was the centre of China's iron and steel industry. It took them several months to dismantle (take apart) all of Anshan's machinery. It was then packed, numbered and crated.' (E)

F Mao Zedong (left) and Chiang Kaishek

Defeating the Guomindang

Now that Japan was defeated there was a real danger of all-out civil war in China between the Nationalists and the Communists. US General George Marshall was sent to China to try to bring about an agreement. Meanwhile the USA continued to supply weapons to Chiang's forces. **F** shows Chiang and Mao meeting for the first time since 1926.

Stalin, the Russian leader, also wanted a civil war to be avoided. Mao later pointed out:

In 1945 Stalin refused to support the cause of revolution in China and said to us: 'Do not have a civil war. Work with Chiang Kaishek. Otherwise China will collapse.' **(G)**

Some historians have suggested that Stalin did not want a Communist take-over of China in case Mao replaced him as the leader of the Communist world.

No agreement could be reached between Mao and Chiang. When the Russians announced that they planned to withdraw from Manchuria both Nationalist and Communist forces moved in. In March 1946 fighting broke out at Shenyang. This was the beginning of a new civil war. To most people Nationalist victory seemed certain. Lobsang had by this time joined the nationalist army because he needed a job. He asks:

How did they (the Guomindang) manage to lose the war? They had something like eight million troops — more than half of them in Manchuria. At that time I doubt if the Communists had more than one million soldiers — unpaid, ragged, badly armed and equipped. Yet within three years it was all over. How?

... nearly everyone in the Guomindang army was on the make. Officers fiddled their accounts, drawing pay for twice the number of men they really commanded, and keeping the extra for themselves. Army stores were sold on the black market. The only things the Guomindang seemed to think of were money, food, drink and women. When soldiers are living like that they don't want to fight and they don't want to die. In any case there was no feeling in the Guomindang that they were fighting for a cause. None of the men in the Guomindang had any respect for their officers. None of the officers respected their generals and the generals didn't respect Chiang Kaishek. The Guomindang army often robbed the local people, taxed them to the hilt and lived off their food. The communists did none of these things . . . (see page 00). *People knew that even in the days before the defeat by Japan, the Communists had been eager to fight the foreign invaders first and their Guomindang enemies afterwards. The Guomindang had done exactly the opposite. The ordinary people had always felt that the Communists were at least fellow Chinese.* **(H)**

To the outside world it seemed that the Nationalists were winning. In March 1947 Nationalist forces took Yanan. This appeared to be a great victory. In fact the Communists had already moved their headquarters out of the city. In Manchuria the Red Army, now calling itself the People's Liberation Army (PLA), smashed the Nationalist forces. The PLA in Manchuria was commanded by Lin Biao. In 1947 Nationalist armies in Changshun and Shenyang (Mukden) were surrounded and cut off. In October 1948, 100 000 Nationalist soldiers in Changshun surrendered. Meanwhile, the Nationalist army in Shenyang tried to break out of the city. Lin Biao's forces attacked them on all sides. After 72 hours the whole of the Shenyang army had been destroyed.

As the civil war raged, the Chinese economy was left in ruins. Inflation went up so fast that prices often doubled within a few hours. People lost their life's savings overnight as money became worthless. **J** shows people outside a bank in Shanghai in 1948.

As map **K** shows, in 1948 and 1949 most of China fell into Communist hands. Nationalist soldiers surrendered in their thousands. In many cases they actually joined the PLA. In January 1949 the Nationalist army

J A 'rush' on a Shanghai bank in 1948

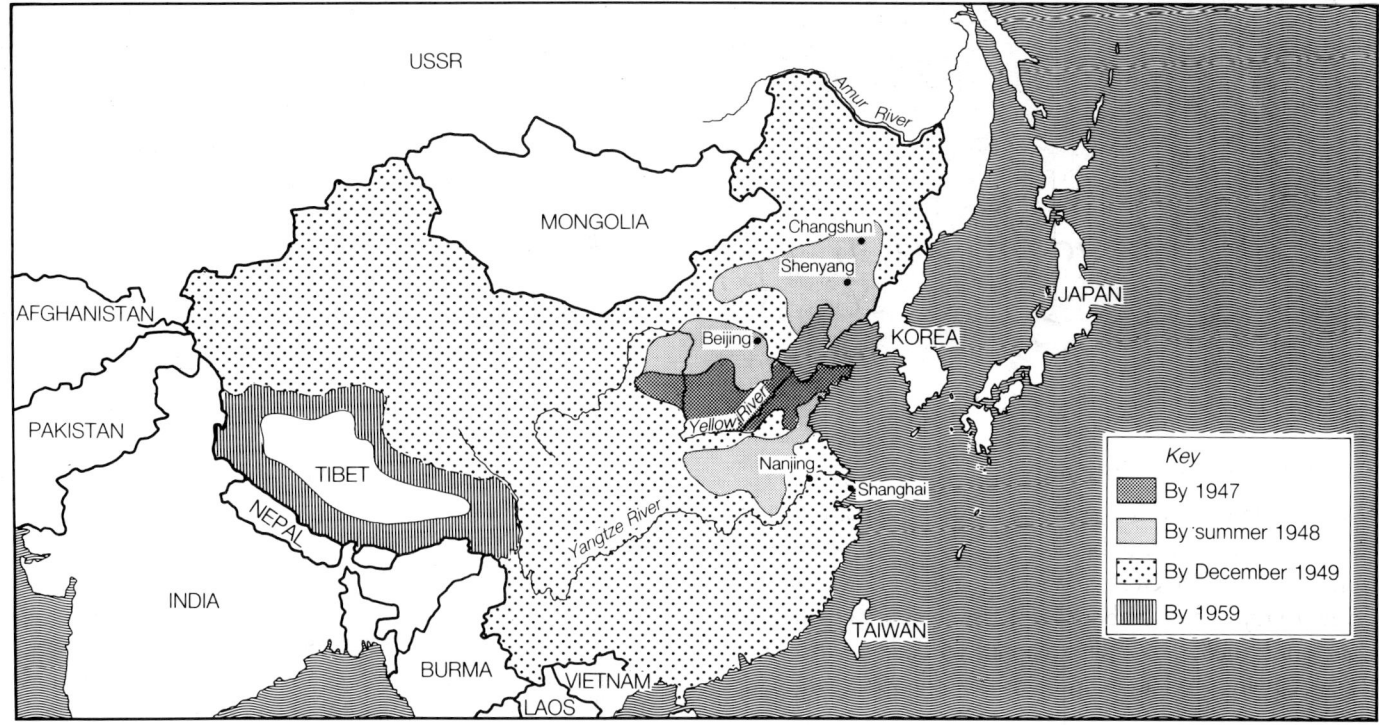

K   The Communist take-over of China

in Beijing gave in without a fight after the officers were told that they could change sides and join the PLA, keeping their old ranks. One of these officers was Lobsang. **L** shows the PLA entering Beijing in 1949. In May 1949 communist troops took Shanghai. A Chinese woman, then a young girl, remembers:

'On the evening of 25 May the radio announced 'Our army of liberation has entered Shanghai'. Like many others, my family gathered around the radio where from time to time music was interrupted by news reports. 'Have no fear, people of Shanghai. Beware of rumours and lies. The People's Liberation Army will take nothing from you, not even a pin. The Red Army is your family.' Suddenly, we could see the troops of the Red Army with our own eyes. They were on our street, moving forward with caution in single file, their rifles fixed with bayonets. They looked nothing like the soldiers of Chiang Kaishek . . . they were much less smart. Their simple padded uniforms, caps and cotton shoes made them seem less frightening.' (**M**)

L   PLA soldiers being welcomed into Beijing

The remains of the Guomindang withdrew to the island of Taiwan. By September 1949 most of mainland China was in the hands of the PLA. China was now a Communist country.

??????????????

1 a How were Britain and the USA brought into the war against Japan?
b How did the British and Americans supply Chiang Kaishek after the Burma Road was closed? How did Chiang use these supplies?
c Use **C** and **D** to explain what the 'Mass Line' was.
d Why did the Russians invade Manchuria?
e What reasons have been given to explain why Stalin did not want a civil war in China? Can you suggest any *other* reasons?

2 What do you think Chiang Kaishek meant in **A**?

3 a Use **H** to explain why the Communists won the civil war.
b How, according to **M** did the PLA try to get public support before they entered big cities such as Shanghai?

4 a **B**, **E**, **G**, **H** and **M** are all based on personal memories. All of them were written down over twenty years after the events they describe. Why must we treat such evidence with extra caution?
b How far can we trust **D**, **G** and **H**?

13 Changes 1

'We announce the setting up of the People's Republic of China. Our nation will from now on enter the large family of peace-loving and freedom-loving nations of the world. It will work bravely to create its own civilisation and happiness and will at the same time promote world peace and freedom. Our nation will never again be insulted. We have stood up.' (A)

These words were spoken by Mao Zedong on 1 October 1949 above the Gate of Heavenly Peace in Beijing. Pages 34–37 look at some of the important changes in everyday life in China during the early years of the People's Republic.

The problems facing the new rulers were huge. For nearly 50 years there had been fighting in China. The country had little industry left. Money had no value. In the towns there was high unemployment and in the countryside there were food shortages. At the same time China's population was going up by about 14 million people a year (see pages 62–63). The task of the government was to rebuild the country while at the same time keeping firm control of the people.

Beijing once again became the capital of China. Mao was now Chairman of the People's Republic and the Prime Minister was Zhou Enlai. Officially the People's Republic was to be ruled by a *coalition* government made up of 14 different parties (all of them very small compared with the Communist Party).

In practice, though, power rested with the leadership of the Communist Party. Ordinary party members obeyed orders from the top. Communist Party officials (or 'cadres') were put in charge at every level of Chinese society: in villages, in towns, in unions, in courts, in colleges, in radio stations and newspapers.

Officially, the People's Republic was a democracy. However, Mao had already pointed out:

'Democracy is practised by the people. The people enjoy the rights of freedom of speech, freedom to meet together, the right to form associations and so on. The right to vote belongs only to the people and not to the reactionaries. There is democracy for the people and dictatorship for the reactionaries. This is the People's Democratic Dictatorship.' (B)

The *reactionaries* were the old landowners and members of the Guomindang. It was the old landlord classes who suffered most with the coming of communism. A land revolution was taking place in the countryside.

Think about the following people. Use the evidence on these pages to work out how each of them might have felt about communist rule. Would you expect them to have been: excited; worried; happy; sad; scared; or unconcerned about it?

Writer: she was arrested by the Guomindang because of her support for the Communist Party. She escaped and worked for several years in Yanan. She was prepared to be critical of the party when she thought it was doing things wrong.

Civil servant: he worked for the Nationalist Government in Nanjing. He stayed on after the Japanese invaded and agreed to work for them. He was put in prison when he refused to execute some Chinese prisoners. After the Second World War he worked for the Guomindang again.

Miner: his family had moved to Datong in 1939 to escape famine. He had been forced to work down the mines with his father by the Japanese. He had seen the Japanese kill his father.

Shanghai woman: she had recently been forced into a marriage which her parents had arranged. Her husband was a rich businessman living in Shanghai.

Businessman: he was one of the richest men in Shanghai. He owned several factories but was always kind to his workers and paid them quite well. He also owned land outside Shanghai but the rents he charged were fairly low. Compared with other landowners peasants thought he was a good landlord.

Landowner: the peasants in the local villages hated him. The rents he charged were very high. He would often evict peasants who fell behind with their rent.

Poor peasant: he had to pay high rents for his land. He had had to sell one of his daughters in order to feed the rest of his family during the last famine. One of his sons fought in the PLA.

Rich peasant: her husband owned some land of his own. The family could not farm all of it so they hired other peasants to work for them. Her family own their house and they are the richest peasants in their village.

Nationalist: she was the widow of Sun Yatsen, the man who founded the Guomindang. She believed that her husband would have wished to continue to work with the communists. She felt that Chiang Kaishek had betrayed the Nationalists.

Steel worker: he had worked in a steel plant in Shenyang, Manchuria. He had been forced to work for the Japanese for low wages. When the Russians invaded he had to help them take the steel works apart and watch it taken to the USSR. For the last three years he had been unemployed. Sometimes his family had had to beg in the streets for food.

The Communist Party needed to keep the support of the peasants. From 1946 onwards the PLA encouraged the peasants to take over the land they had liberated. The slogan of the Party was 'Land to the Tiller'. In 1950 Mao's government passed the Agrarian Reform Law. In 1927 he had written:

> *Local bullies and evil landowners have killed peasants without batting an eyelid. In view of these crimes, how can anyone say that the peasants should not now rise and shoot one or two of them, and bring about a small-scale reign of terror in crushing these people.* (C)

Party officials were sent into villages all over China to help with land reform. Land, animals and stores of grain were taken from the landlords and given to the peasants. Peasants were encouraged to put their landlords and sometimes the richer peasants on trial in 'People's Courts' (D). A famous Chinese writer, Ding Ling, described what happened in the People's Courts:

> *Qian (the landlord) knelt in the middle of the stage. He read: 'In the past I committed crimes in the village, making life miserable for the good people . . .'*
>
> *'That won't do! Just to write 'I' won't do! Write 'local tyrant' (bad ruler) Qian.'*
>
> *The wicked Qian began to read again: 'I Qian, a local tyrant, committed crimes in the village, making life miserable for good people, and I deserve to die a hundred times over; but my good friends are merciful . . .'*
>
> *'Who the devil are you calling your good friends? Say all the poor gentlemen.'*
>
> *Qian had to continue: 'Thanks to the mercy of all the poor gentlemen of the village . . .'*
>
> *'That's no good. Don't say poor gentlemen; today we poor people have stood up. Say "the liberated gentlemen!"'*
>
> *'Thanks to the mercy of the liberated gentlemen my life has been spared . . .'*
>
> *'What? I don't understand.' Another voice from the crowd interrupted Qian. 'We liberated gentlemen aren't going to accept all this posh stuff. Just put it briefly: says your dog's life has been spared.'*
>
> *Qian had to go on: 'Spare my dog's life. In future I must change my past evil ways completely. If I . . . go against the people in any way. I shall be put to death.'* (E)

Qian was lucky. Many landlords and sometimes their families — perhaps as many as one million of them — were executed. Others were sent to prison or to special camps to be 're-educated'. Those who had been good landlords were simply given a share of the land along with the peasants. The land revolution was completed by the end of 1951. The People's Courts had destroyed the old landowning classes. The biggest threat inside China to the new Communist Government had been removed.

?????????????

1 a What do you think Mao meant in **A** when he said 'We have stood up'?
b How many parties were officially in the new government?
c What was the 'People's Democratic Dictatorship'?
d What was the 'Agrarian Reform Law'?

2 *Role play.* In groups or as a class act out a 'People's Court' trial. You need people to play these roles: Chairman; Communist Party official; accusers; landlord; witnesses; hecklers (people who call out as the peasants did to Qian).

D A landlord on trial before a 'people's court'

14 Changes 2

H Why do you think portraits of Chairman Mao were put up in classrooms?

At first change in the towns and cities was slow compared with change in the country. Chow Qingli, the wife of a businessman in Shanghai, describes some of the changes she saw:

❛*Mao Zedong's picture, along with pictures of Zhu De and Zhou Enlai, began appearing all over the streets of Shanghai. More and more people were dressing in the same blue 'Mao-suits'.*

Within three years of the Liberation, life in cities like Shanghai was completely different. The teachers, missionaries, bankers and businessmen from Europe and America were now only a memory . . . The big foreign cars had gone. Instead vast numbers of bicycles had appeared. All of China's people, from old men to children, had begun a big clean up – against rats, flies and mosquitoes. Each family was asked to produce a weekly number of rat tails, at least one rat tail per member of the family. Those who beat the required number were allowed to have a small red flag on their front door. Soon there were red flags all over the place.

Another change was that beggars disappeared almost overnight. Before 1949 they had been a normal sight at every street corner.

One of the most dramatic changes that took place, and one that made me weep bitterly was Mao's Marriage Reform Law. This came only five months after my own (forced) marriage.❜ (A)

This is what the Marriage Reform Law of 1950 said:

❛*The old marriage system which allowed forced or arranged marriages and which made women the servants of their men is now abolished. All marriages are to be based on the free consent of men and women.*❜ (B)

Divorce was made easier. Many women were now able to divorce their husbands. Chow Qingli goes on:

❛*Mao also banned other horrible practices such as the drowning of newborn female babies, polygamy (having more than one wife) and the selling of women as servants or prostitutes. Mass meetings and campaigns were held through-*

out the city to explain the laws. I myself went to some of these meetings. At the same time secret societies and some religious orders were coming under attack in the cities. Many of these were very corrupt anyway. Each government decision at once became the subject of endless discussion, not only in the newspapers and on the radio, but also on the walls of the city. (C)

One of the government's decisions was to bring inflation under control by fixing prices and wages. As a result many businesses went bankrupt. All private banks were closed down and a new state bank was set up. Companies could only borrow money from this bank if they had the support of the Communist Party. Chow Qingli points out:

In general those who had most reason to fear the PLA – the warlords, bankers and corrupt officials – had already fled to Taiwan. Those who stayed behind found at first that they could carry on with business as usual. The government badly wanted to persuade the capitalists (businessmen) *to start to rebuild.* (D)

This policy of allowing small businesses to continue was called 'limited capitalism'. Chow says:

I myself was one of the richest women in Shanghai. The government needed the money and expert knowledge of businessmen. In fact when the workers of a foreign electric company started to make demands of the management, the government ordered the workers to stop doing this and obey the company's orders. After all, that company happened to supply all the electricity for Shanghai's trams! (E)

Meanwhile China was again caught up in war. In June 1950 North Korea, with Russian backing, invaded South Korea. When the North Koreans were driven back by US and UN troops, Chinese forces became involved in the fighting. Inside the People's Republic the government moved against people it thought might be enemies of communism. These enemies included those who had worked for the Japanese, ex-Guomindang officials and some businessmen. The 'Three Antis Campaign' was started against corruption, waste and *bureaucracy* (red-tape). Chow tells us:

A wave of attacks against enemies of the Revolution broke out over the city of Shanghai. During the month of April alone, there were countless police raids as well as huge public trials. When these ended the newspapers published lists of those who were to be executed. Hundreds were shot that same afternoon on the golf course to the west of Shanghai.

In 1953 a new stage in the Liberation brought all private businesses under government control. When my husband's company was taken over he continued to hold the post of manager, under the eye of a trade unionist. Changes of this sort were always followed by a process of 're-education'. This meant compulsory meetings two or three times a week. People were made to criticise themselves and the things they had done in the past, and criticise each other as well. Also, the works of Marx, Lenin and Stalin. The writings of Mao Zedong became like scripture. (F)

Chow goes on:

The government then started the Campaign of Five Antis. This attacked the crimes of bribery, not paying your taxes, fraud, taking government property and spying . . . those found guilty were usually sent to labour camps to be re-educated, rather than corporal punishment or execution. Even so many wealthy people committed suicide at this time. They could not stand the idea of a public trial. (G)

'Re-education' was part of the process of 'thought reform', by which everyone learned about communist beliefs. Marxism was taught in schools and colleges, as well as in the study groups mentioned in **F**. **H** shows children in school, with a poster of Mao Zedong. Newspapers and radio had been under direct party control since 1949.

People who spoke out publicly against the new order could find themselves in real trouble. These *dissidents* were sent to labour camps to be re-educated. Sometimes they were sent into the countryside to be reformed by learning the ways of the peasants.

??????????????

1 a How did the new government go about getting the streets of Shanghai and other cities cleaned up?
b How did women benefit from the Marriage Reform Law?
c How did the Communist government deal with inflation?
d What was 'limited capitalism'?
e What reasons are given in **E** to explain why the government did not take over all private businesses straight away?
f What were: the 'Three Antis Campaign', and the 'Five Antis Campaign'?

2 a Use the evidence in **A**, **C**, **F**, **G** and **H** to describe how the Communist Party tried to get public support.
b What do you think Chow meant by saying 'the writings of Mao became like scripture' (**F**)?

3 Either: draw a series of cartoons showing how life in China was changing,
or: as though you are a member of the Communist Party, write a letter to a friend in Hong Kong describing the changes that are taking place.

15 Five Year Plan: Industry 1953–7

'The town of Fushun was a good example of the growing industrial towns – a city of 700 000 people that was four times as big as it had been in 1949. It had three underground mines as well as another three petrol plants on the way. The secretary of the town government was a young woman. We sat around with the usual cups of green tea while she fired off the figures: 19 new clinics, 11 more schools, and five more 'improvement' centres. The next day we drove on even deeper into Manchuria. The train ride to Anshan was fantastic. It was like looking at the surface of the Moon, made up of new bricks and drifting smoke, bridges with many guards, great gangs and communities of people laying huge girders (beams) over river beds.' (A)

James Cameron, a British reporter, wrote **A** in 1954. This was just one year into China's *Five Year Plan*. The aim of this Plan, which lasted from 1953 to 1957, was to build up China's industries as fast as possible.

Between 1953 and 1957 Chinese industries grew faster than those of any other country in history. The number of people living in big cities went up by over 20 million.

The Chinese government wanted to change China from a backward peasant society into a great modern industrial country. The Five Year Plan of 1953–7 was to be the first stage of this change. By making more and more of everything, China would become a much richer country. The standard of living would go up and the number of very poor people would go down. Karl Marx had said that communism could only be brought about in a rich industrial society (see pages 14–15), not one where millions of people were struggling just to stay alive. By building up the industries of the country, the communists believed that the People's Republic of China would become one of the most powerful countries in the world.

In late 1949, Mao visited Moscow. He stayed for nine weeks. In February 1950 the People's Republic of China and the USSR made a treaty of friendship. Stalin, the Russian leader, agreed to give China 300 million US dollars in aid over the next five years. In fact this was really a very small sum of money. Even so, when Mao left Moscow he said the friendship between the People's Republic and the USSR was:

'everlasting and could never be destroyed!' (B)

C is a Chinese poster showing the friendship between the people of the USSR and China.

In the 1920s and 1930s Stalin's policies had turned the USSR from a backward country of peasants into one of the most powerful industrial countries in the world. The Five Year Plan was China's attempt to copy the Soviet example.

The USSR sent 10 000 scientists and other experts to help with the Five Year Plan. 694 important industrial projects were started in 1953. These included building iron and steel plants, sinking mines, starting chemical works and building huge factories for making 'Liberation' lorries, trains, planes and other transport. Of these 694 projects, 156 of the most important ones were designed and built by Russians. Russian scientists were in control of them. Many Chinese people did not like having to work under the Russians. Thousands of Chinese students were sent to the USSR to be trained.

Few of the new industries were built in China's existing big cities. Instead they were started in smaller cities and towns such as Baotou, Lanzhou, Wuhan, Zhengzhou and Luoyang. Wuhan, for instances, became a huge iron and steel making area in the space of just five years. In 1939 a top geologist working for the Nationalist Government had said China had so few iron ore reserves that:

'It is quite clear that China can never become an iron-producing country of any importance.' (D)

By 1957 huge iron reserves had been found in north west China, the biggest being in Gansu province. Meanwhile vast oil reserves had been found in Sichuan.

To get people to work as hard and as long as possible, special bonus schemes were started. Workers were paid according to how hard they worked and according to the

C A wall poster showing friendship between China and Russia

E Production under the first five year plan

Product	1952	1957 (planned)	1957 (achieved)
Coal (million tons)	63.5	113	124
Pig-iron (million tons)	1.9	4.7	5.86
Steel (million tons)	1.35	4.12	5.24
Chemical Fertilizer (thousand tons)	194	570	740
Machine-tools (pieces)	13734	37192	80000 (1958)
Crude oil (million tons)	0.44	2	1.42
Cement (million tons)	2.6	6	4.65
Electric Power (thousand million kilowatt)	7.26	15.9	19.1

standard of their work. Some became 'model' workers because of their efforts and were made famous in newspapers and on wall posters throughout the towns and cities of China. This was meant to give other workers a standard to aim for. It worked, for by 1956 most of the targets in the Five Year Plan for heavy industry had been beaten (see **E**). These figures came from the Chinese Government. C.K. Yang, an American professor who lived in China in the early 1950s, writes:

There is a problem in using information provided by the Communists. They give you a mass of figures which often say different things. There is little chance of being able to check on them. (**F**)

Under the Five Year Plan new railway lines were started, together with projects to build new roads. China would need a better railway system to transport materials and goods to and from the new industrial towns. In the past, one of the reasons why parts of China had fallen under the control of warlords was because Beijing was so far away from them. A better transport system would also mean that the new Communist Government would have more control over what went on in the most remote parts of the country. **G** shows the main railway lines in China. Many of these lines were started during the Five Year Plan of 1953–7. Great new bridges were also built. One of the most famous of these bridges was the Yangtze River Bridge. It is 6700 metres long with a double railway track and a wide road. It was opened in 1954.

There were big advances in education too. In 1949 only one in ten people could read and write. By the end of the Five Year Plan one in four could read and write, and most villages had their own primary schools, usually built by the villagers themselves. Often pupils, on their return from school, would teach their parents what they had learned that day. In this way more and more adults learned to read and write.

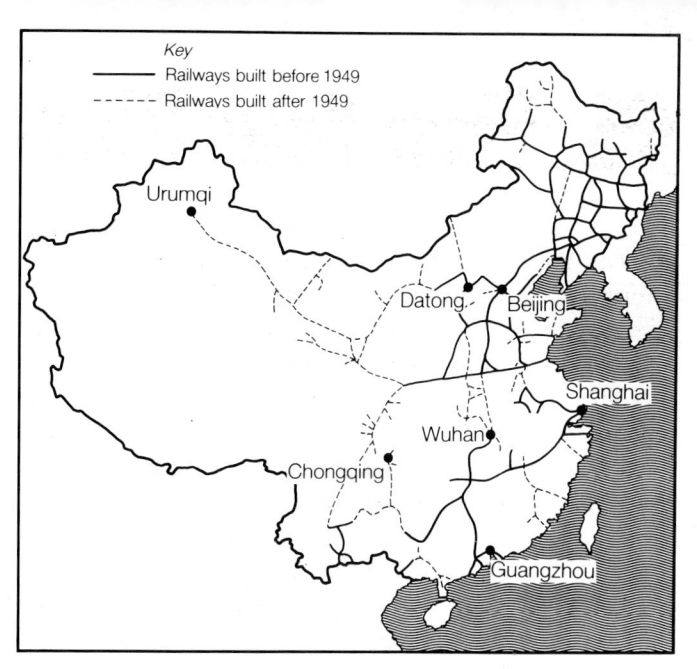

G The Chinese railway network

The number of people living in towns and cities went up very fast. In 1952 about 71 million people were living in the towns. By 1957 there were 92 million. These extra townspeople had to be fed, along with all the other people working on industrial projects. China's population was growing by 14 million people a year, which meant another 14 million mouths to be fed. The Five Year Plan for industry was only a success because food production went up at the same time. The years 1953–7 saw big changes in the ways that peasants lived and worked. Not all of these changes were popular, as the next section shows.

??????????????????

1 a What was the main aim of the Five Year Plan?
b Why did the government want to turn China into an industrial country?
c Why did it make sense for China to try to copy Soviet methods of building up their industries?

2 a Where did James Cameron get his figures from (**A**)?
b What problem is there in using figures from Chinese Government sources (**F**)?
c Look at **B**. From what you have read on these pages explain what problems China would face if Mao were to be proved wrong and the 'friendship' ended.

3 What message is poster **C** trying to get across? Why do you think the artist drew the boy at the front holding a toy aeroplane?

16 Farming and the Five Year Plan

Land Reform had given the land to the peasants. This did not mean that the peasants produced more food. Each peasant family simply farmed its own small plots, trying to grow enough for themselves, and in a good year growing a bit extra to sell in the towns. As we saw in the last chapter this was no longer enough. Large amounts of surplus food were now needed. The peasants would have to produce more.

In 1952 Communist Party officials started to encourage villages all over China to set up *Mutual-Aid Teams*. These were already common in parts of north China where the Communists had been in control before 1949. A peasant in south China told an American visitor about the mutual-aid teams:

'Our team is made up of seven families, all poor peasants and before that farm labourers. We faced a shortage of labour during the busy seasons and we were too poor to afford hired help. We were also short of farm tools and too poor to buy fertilizer . . . So we set up our mutual-aid team. We pooled our labour and farm tools for common use. Every family started to collect fertilizer, solving that problem. The Autumn crop was a bumper one, and we had surplus grain to buy tools and fertilizer. This year we plan to produce 20 per cent more wheat. We also plan to start breeding pigs and hens and reclaim some waste land to increase our crop area.' (A)

Each family was rewarded according to how much of the land was theirs, how many of the tools and animals were theirs and how hard they had worked.

In fact peasants had often worked together in this way before the Communist Revolution, especially during times of food shortages. There is also evidence that at this time government officials started telling villagers exactly what they should do. This was something new. Here is a directive from the Guangzhou Area government to party officials in 1953:

'Party members should tell villagers stories about the model labourers and how much they have produced. This will help to get the villagers to work harder.

For this year's spring planting all districts have held peasant representative conferences. These have made up production plans for the year and worked out exactly what they will be doing to produce the spring crop.

The earth work for all the dykes must be finished by the end of March and the dams must be completed by 10 April. All peasants must collect more fertilizer, aiming to collect at least 20 per cent more. Pest control committees must be set up in the villages . . .' (B)

F A production team working on the grain harvest

G   A young tea-picker

Under the mutual-aid teams land was still privately owned by the peasants. This could lead to problems. Another peasant tells us:

In 1951 we set up a mutual-aid team. The work went well, but there were lots of quarrels about whose land should be worked on first. It was difficult to solve all these problems. Some said: 'Why should his field be taken first? I've got a bigger crop. It ought to be my turn now.' Whatever we did this went on. So then we began to talk about forming a peasants' co-operative. (C)

Party officials started trying to get peasants to form peasant co-operatives in 1953. To start a co-operative several mutual-aid teams were joined together. The co-operatives were each run by a committee of peasants, guided by a Party official. The land was pooled together and usually a single crop was grown on all the land. In the early co-operatives the land was still privately owned. By the end of 1954 there were 650 000 co-operatives in China. This may sound a lot but it only covered 15 per cent of China's population. In July 1955 Mao said in a speech:

This is China's position. There is a large population with not enough land being farmed. Natural disasters and famine often hit us and farming methods are backward. As a result, although land reform has greatly helped the lives of the peasants, many people still face hardship. Only a small number of peasants are well off. Some poor peasants have been forced to sell up in order to survive. They now have to work as labourers again. So there is a great need to increase the numbers of co-operatives. (D)

E is from a book the Communist Party published in 1956:

In China 1955 was the year things were decided. The first half of the year was a dark time. But in the second half this all changed. Tens of millions of peasant families swung into action. At the call of the Party Central Committee they formed co-operatives. As this is being written over 60 million peasant families in all parts of the country have already joined co-operatives. By the end of the year the forces of communism will have won another great victory. (E)

In fact many peasants were strongly against joining co-operatives. This was because from 1954 onwards in most co-operatives the peasants no longer owned their own land. It was all taken over by the co-operative, apart from small private plots. Most of the co-operatives were also very big, sometimes with more than 600 peasants in them. Peasants worked in production teams like the peasants in F and G. They were rewarded according to how well they worked.

The land was now collectively owned. Zhou Enlai, the Prime Minister, reported:

By the end of June 1956, 922 000 co-operatives have been set up throughout the country. Their members make up 91.7 per cent of the country's peasant families. (H)

Government sources show what happened to food production (see J). It did not go up as fast as had been expected. This may have been because in 1956 much of China suffered very bad weather. In some areas there

J   Food production in China, 1949–57

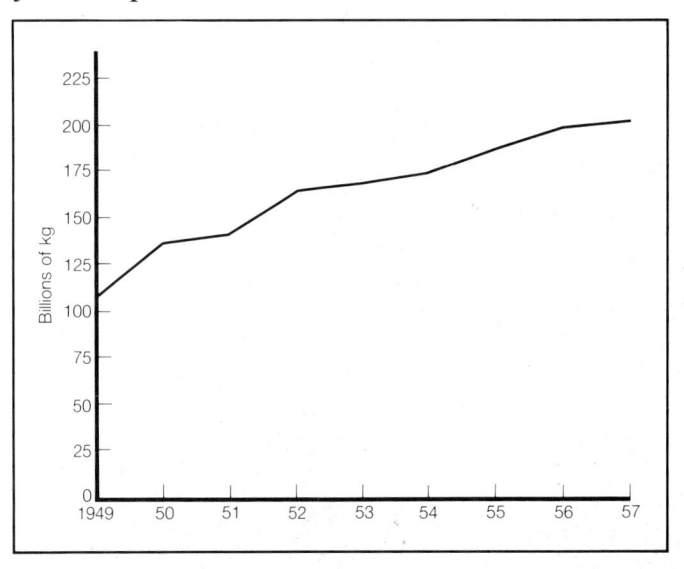

L Rice fields

was no rain, in others there were floods. Millions of peasants left their villages and went to the cities. Many peasants blamed the co-operatives for their problems. **K** is a report from one co-operative team leader in 1956:

'In my co-operative, production has gone down and the members have many different views as to why this has happened. How can I be expected to talk about co-operatives being better?' (**K**)

The aim of the co-operatives was to produce much more food, by farming on a large scale, by using better methods and by reclaiming land. **L** shows rice fields around Chonqing. Over 80 per cent of the surplus food the peasants grew (the food that they did not need to keep for themselves) had to be sold to the government at fixed prices. These prices were very low. This meant that peasants had little reason to try to produce more food. By the end of the Five Year Plan in 1957 China's industrial production was up by 120 per cent. Food production was only up by 25 per cent.

In setting up co-operatives and ending private ownership of the land, the Chinese government was once again copying the Soviet example. However, the position of the USSR after the Russian Revolution (1917) and China's position in the 1950s were very different. Russian peasants had been forced into collective farms so that farm machines could be used and fewer peasants would be needed on the land. The Russian peasants that were no longer of use on the farms went off to the cities where more workers were needed to build the USSR's industries. In China there were very few machines to use on the new large-scale farms. In any case there was no point in getting machines to take over the work of more and more peasants, because there was just not enough work for them to do in the cities. It might seem that the easy way to end this problem would be simply to start new industrial projects. However the Government did not have the money to do this.

Mao Zedong and other Chinese leaders were coming to believe that Soviet methods were no good for dealing with China's problems. As the next pages show, Chinese leaders were about to reject the USSR's way of doing things and start building a very different kind of society. This was to split the Communist world in two.

?????????????????

1 a What were mutual-aid teams?
b How were peasants rewarded in the mutual-aid teams?
c In what ways were co-operatives different from mutual-aid teams?
d Why did Mao think that most peasants would want co-operatives?
e Why didn't production of food rise as quickly as had been expected?
f In which year did food production go up fastest (**J**)?

2 Which of the sources on these pages can we trust? Draw up a chart like the one below and fill it in with your ideas. (Make sure you leave enough space for each source.)

Source	Type of evidence	What it tells us	Reasons for trusting/not trusting it
A			
B			
C			
D			
E			
F			
G			(Is the photographer trying to say something?)
H			
J K L			

3 If you interviewed one of the workers in **F** or the tea-picker in **G**, what might he or she say about the *good* points of co-operatives? What *bad* points might he or she mention?

17 Communes

How would you feel if the local council told you and your family to move out of your home, and sent you to live in army-like barracks, along with hundreds of others? Millions of Chinese peasants found themselves in just this position in 1958.

The Hundred Flowers

By 1956 Mao Zedong and other Chinese leaders were looking for a new way to strengthen communism in China. Mao made a speech in which he said *'let a hundred flowers bloom'*. He asked for open public discussion of China's problems and the way the country was run. He got it. Soon wall posters criticising the government were being stuck up in many towns and cities. Newspapers carried stories attacking the Party. In some cities there were student protests.

Officially the Communist Party was still in a coalition government with other democratic parties. Some members of these parties now demanded the right to form 'opposition parties'.

On 8 June 1957 the Hundred Flowers period ended as suddenly as it had begun. Known critics of the government were arrested. Some were sent off for re-education in the countryside, some were *demoted* (lost their rank), and others lost their jobs. Historians still argue about why the Hundred Flowers took place. It could be that Mao did not realise just how many people were against the Communists. Or perhaps it was simply an easy way for the Communist Party leaders to find out who their critics were, so that they could be arrested.

The Great Leap Forward

In 1958 Mao announced the beginning of the 'Great Leap Forward'. Officially this was China's second Five Year Plan. It was a big change in policy from the first one. China was no longer following the Soviet example. The aim of the Great Leap Forward was to build a modern industrial state by making full use of the peasants. Instead of new large-scale industrial plants being started in the towns, peasants were encouraged to set up their own industries in the villages. This was cheaper than developing bigger towns and cities, and it would overcome the problem of having to transport food supplies.

In the spring of 1958 some co-operatives in Henan joined together to form a *commune* of 40 000 people. By the autumn nearly all of the 750 000 co-operatives in China had been joined together to form 26 000 communes. The communes were on average 30 times the size of the old co-operatives and they worked very differently. Each commune was responsible for running the farming in its area. On 23 September 1958 the *Beijing Review* reported:

'All the means of production (land, tools etc) of the co-operatives are being turned over to the common ownership of the commune, including all the small private vegetable patches. Houses and animals will also now be owned by the communes.' (A)

An Australian who taught in China remembers a talk he had with one of his pupils, a peasant boy:

'Weren't the peasants angry when the Party took away the land that it had given them at the time of land reform?' I asked him.
'They didn't take it away. The commune land belongs to all the commune members. It's not state-owned.'
'But don't the peasants want private land?'
'Some of the rich ones do. They don't like the communes . . .'
'But I mean the poor peasants. The Party gave them the land and then turned it into commune land.'
'Most of the poor peasants know that they can produce more from the land if they share what they have. They see that people don't starve any more. Of course there are a few who would prefer to own land, but not many. The Party is trying to educate them.' (B)

A Party member tells us how his co-operative joined a commune:

'Some people said (a commune) was not needed. They said: 'Why should we change everything again now? Things are going well as they are . . .
But we discussed it and put over the Party's view. The Party had said that communes were supposed to make better use of manpower, to help develop industries. After we had put over the Party's views we joined the Liu Ling People's Commune.' (C)

Communes meant that farming could be done on an even bigger scale. It was thought this would lead to a rise in production. Each commune was also meant to start new local industries as part of the Great Leap Forward. The same Party member tells us:

'. . . we experimented making our own iron by our own local method. We have of course both coal and iron ore up in the hills. We built a blast furnance and I was responsible for organising the work. There were 70 of us working on this but as far as I can remember it didn't pay.' (D)

Each commune was divided up into brigades of about 600 people, depending on the size of the commune. Each brigade was made up of production teams of up to 200 people. **E** shows a production team at work.

For several years, life for millions of Chinese peasants became rather like life in the army. Instead of eating in

E A production team from a 'model brigade'

their own homes peasants now had to eat in canteens run by the communes. This meant that fewer women were needed for cooking, so more women could do other kinds of work. In some communes family houses were knocked down and everyone had to live in barracks, with men and women sleeping in different blocks.

Each commune was meant to be self-supporting, as far as possible. They ran their own schools and nurseries, so women could spend less time in child care and more time working on the land or in local industries. Special homes were set up for old people and they too were given work to do. Communes also set up their own health services. The aim was to get *everyone* working to build communism. Major projects were started to control water supplies. Millions more areas of land were irrigated. Dams and reservoirs were built in an effort to deal with droughts and floods.

Some communes were held up as *models* or examples for all the others to copy. The most famous of these was the Dazhai Commune, which became known all over the world in the 1960s (see pages 46–47).

At first it seemed that the Great Leap Forward was a success. In the autumn of 1958 Mao Zedong said that the country's grain production had nearly doubled and he expected it to double again in the following year. Production of pig iron went shooting up. But the figures are misleading. Although pig iron production doubled as a result of the backyard furnaces, most of it was such poor quality that it was useless. Worse than that, grain production did not go up as quickly as Mao claimed.

In some communes peasants were now doing less work than before, because they were no longer being paid according to how much they did. Instead all members were getting the same wages. In other communes peasants were told to take on new farming methods which were being used in some of the model communes, even if they knew the new methods were wrong for their kind of land. One peasant later explained how his production team changed the levels of water in their rice fields:

❝*Before the water in the paddy fields used to be above the ankle, now it went above the knee. But deep down the soil is no good. Only four or five inches on the top are good. It wasn't right but we couldn't help it. We got orders.*❞ **(F)**

As well as this many peasants worked in the new small scale industries and not on the land. During the autumn of 1958 under half of all peasants were working on the land. Food production turned out to be well short of government targets. The Great Leap Forward had failed.

In December 1958 Mao gave up being President of the People's Republic, although he remained Chairman of the Communist Party. Some historians believe Mao was forced to resign. Liu Shaoqi became the new President. Early in 1960 the Great Leap Forward was called off.

Communes were re-organised and made smaller: in 1962 there were 76 000 communes in China, in 1958 there had been just 26 000. The land was now owned by the production teams rather than the communes. The peasants were given back their own small private plots for growing vegetables. In many communes the canteens were closed down. Once again peasants were paid according to how much work they did. The same Australian teacher tells us how this was done:

❝*Their income is now calculated by the number of work points they collect during the year. These work points are checked at meetings in which all commune members take part. Each peasant says how many work points he thinks he has earned and the others then say whether they agree or disagree with his figures. . . . it is very rare indeed for the others to lower the figure . . . Each peasant can spend his income as he wants for he does not have to pay taxes. Instead the commune pays 60 per cent of all that it produces to the government.*❞ **(G)**

However the Great Leap Forward had done its damage. When in 1960 some parts of China were hit by drought and other parts by floods, it was clear that China was heading for disaster.

18 Famine

Between 1960 and 1962 famine hit China. This was due mainly to the bad weather. In some parts of China there were floods, in other parts drought. There were also a series of *typhoons* (hurricanes). The outside world knew there were food shortages because the Chinese had to import food. But few people outside China knew just how bad the disaster was.

We can get some idea of what happened from the memories of ordinary Chinese people. Here is one such account:

It was in 1960 that all China fell on hard times. I was almost seven. Rice, cooking oil and soya beans were strictly rationed. Meat, eggs, flour and sugar disappeared completely. The cost of fresh vegetables went out of sight . . . We were always hungry.

Father explained that the rivers and lakes had overflowed and the peasants couldn't grow anything for us to eat. 'But you're lucky,' he said. 'You live in a big capital city, and the Party and Chairman Mao are giving you food from the storage bins. The peasants have to find a way out for themselves.'

I got used to going with my sisters to the Martyrs' Park to pull up a kind of wild grass that could be made into a paste with broken grains of rice and steamed and eaten as 'bittercakes'. In the end even this was in short supply . . .

Many of the old people and almost all the children I knew had the 'water swelling disease' dropsy. Our bodies puffed up and wouldn't get better. Each day we would walk slowly to school and arrive exhausted. When friends met each other, they squeezed each others' legs to see how swollen they were and examined each others' skins to see if they were yellow . . .

One day Father came home very quiet and depressed . . . Finally he told us that at a commune in Hengyang District to the south, nearly a whole production team had died of hunger, and there was no one left with enough strength to bury the bodies. They were still lying scattered about in the fields from which they had been trying to pull up enough food to stay alive.

By the second year my nan's condition was very bad because she often gave away the small share of food that was hers. Father used his reporter's card (he worked for the Hunan Daily) to buy a pound of sugar and a pound of sweets for her every month at a special store for Party officials. But she would pass it on to us secretly, saying, 'Eat it so you won't be sick. You still have a lot of growing to do.' Then one day when we all got up my nan stayed in bed. She slept so long that in the end we went up to wake her, but she wouldn't wake up . . .

Later the writer went to live in the countryside:

The peasants were very nice to us, bringing out a special tea I had never tasted before, made with soya beans, sesame seeds, salt and ginger. Then they served dinner . . . There was no meat, but they brought out a small dish of smoked fish. The rest was gourds (a fruit) and cabbage, dishes which were to be our main food for months.

Firewood had been a big problem in the countryside since the Great Leap Forward. Chairman Mao had ordered the peasants to stop working the fields and cut down the big trees to run iron and steel furnaces. Now there was little fuel left except for the brushwood and grass on the mountainsides. It was always difficult to keep the kitchen fire going under the stove.
(A)

The flooding in North China may partly have been caused by the Chinese themselves. So much land had been irrigated that the *water table* (water level) in parts of North China was raised and the land flooded more easily. Floods ruined millions of acres of pasture land and wheat-growing areas. Food was brought in from Australia and Canada. It is difficult to judge just how many people in China died in the famine. But one thing is certain: the big improvements made in farming in the 1950s saved millions more Chinese people from starving to death.

??????????????

1 a What was the Hundred Flowers Campaign?
b What reasons have been put forward to explain why it took place?
c What was the aim of the Great Leap Forward?

2 a What were the main causes of famine in China in the early 1960s?
b How might the improved farming methods have added to the problem?

3 Imagine you are at a meeting about setting up a commune. Write down what you would like to say *against* joining the commune. Would you have the courage to say it?

19 Communes: Two Examples

These pages look at two very different communes. One was in Inner Mongolia and the other at Dazhai in Shanxi. Colin Mackerras, who lived in China in the 1960s, visited these two communes and later wrote about what he saw (**A** and **B**):

A commune in Inner Mongolia

It was by far the poorest commune I saw in China and very few foreigners go there. The whole commune is made up of 4000 families and has a total population of 16 000 people, grouped in 32 villages and 25 brigades. The main crop is maize. As in other areas of North China no rice is grown. Many sheep are kept for their wool, meat and the clothes that can be made from their skins.

There is special help for the old and peasants who need medical treatment are sent to a hospital in the city. 80 per cent of the land is irrigated and 60 per cent is ploughed with tractors . . . There is electricity for water pumps and for people's homes. The water pumps are very important for irrigation because droughts are common. I think the reason why I was shown this commune was so that they could 'show off' these water pumps.

Some brigades have nurseries but others do not, so that many women do not work in the fields because they have to look after their children. There are 19 primary schools for the 2500 children. There is also one secondary school. Not all children go to school.

'What do the other children do, the ones who don't got to school?', I asked the commune leader.

'Oh, mostly they help to look after their younger brothers and sisters.'

'Can't they go to school if they want to?'

'Well it's the parents who decide. The commune gives every child the chance to have a primary education . . . Some parents say there is too much work to be done in the home. After all, 20 years ago none of the poor peasants would even have dreamed of education. It takes them quite a time to get used to it.'

Medical services were about the worst I saw in China. 'We have only one clinic' the commune leader told me, 'but we have ten doctors and nurses who travel round from brigade to brigade looking after the sick.'

'Do many babies die while still very young?' I asked him.

'Hardly any. Before liberation about one in three children died in the first year of life. But we are still short of doctors and medical supplies.' (**A**)

Dazhai

In the 1960s the villagers of Dazhai became a model commune. They were held up as an example to all of China. Foreigners were encouraged to go there to see what commune life was meant to be like. Colin Mackerras tells us:

The fame of Dazhai is to be seen from the fact that in every Chinese village the slogan 'learn from Dazhai' can be seen in large letters on the walls. It is famous because of the way its 365 people have set an example by carving out terraced fields from steep stony hillsides. They have done this through sheer hard work using only simple tools. The whole place is only 500 acres, 133 of which are now being farmed. In 1963 terrible rains poured down, destroying the fields and the peasants' houses. They decided to re-build the terraces without asking for any help from the government. They worked through the winter, often in heavy snow. In the evenings they re-built their houses.

I saw a peasant ploughing one of the terraced hills with an ox-drawn wooden plough. Behind him another scattered seed, while a third spread manure. The fields are irrigated mainly by hand. To educate the young, sections of the land are kept just as they used to be. There is a big difference.

The new houses of Dazhai are all in one long two-floored block, built of stone. Each house is the same, including that of

C Posters like this encouraged other communes to copy Dazhai

D Using 'walking tractors' to cultivate fields at Dazhai

Chen Yonggui (the brigade leader). The peasants' houses have both electricity and running water. Running water in a Chinese peasant's home is rare.
'Doesn't it interfere with your daily work having visitors coming here from all over China?', I asked Chen.
'No! Only a few people are needed to show them round.'
'Doesn't it make them big-headed to know that the whole country is learning from them?'
'There is a risk of that, but you've seen other communes. You can see how poor this place still is.'

Chen was right! Dazhai is very poor in many ways, but there is no doubt that it is progressing very fast! It has a special feeling about it, a real sense of community and pride in what has been achieved.
'It is because we study Chairman Mao's works' said a young Dazhai peasant. '(He) teaches us not to fear difficulties or hard work. He also tells us the need to serve the people and look at problems in a scientific way.'

'Not to fear difficulties or hard work'. This is what the Chinese mean when they talk about the Spirit of Dazhai. It is very much needed in a country like China, where there are still very few farming machines. It is clear that Chinese peasants are still very poor, but they are not as poor as they used to be and things are still getting better. So it is hardly surprising that most of them support the government. **(B)**

C is a famous poster showing the people of Dazhai at work. D shows them in the fields. Millions of people came from all over China to visit Dazhai. Chen Yonggui went on to be a member of the Chinese *Politburo* (cabinet).

However in 1982 Fox Butterfield, a New York Times reporter in Beijing wrote:

'In 1980 the government admitted that Dazhai was a fraud. The 'People's Daily' confessed that Dazhai had not really relied on its own efforts to terrace rocky hills and dig its irrigation ditches. The truth was that Dazhai had accepted millions of dollars in government aid and the help of thousands of soldiers. Dazhai's ever-increasing grain production figures were a fake too . . . The production of grain had really gone down year by year. Not only that, Chen Yonggui had executed 141 people during the mid 1960s.' **(E)**

??????????????

1 a What machines were being used in the commune described in **A**?
b Why did Mackerras think he had been shown *that* commune rather than another one?
c Why didn't some of the children at the commune in **A** go to school? Do you think the commune should have made them go?
d In what other ways had life improved for peasants in that part of Inner Mongolia since Liberation?

2 a In what ways did Dazhai turn out to be a fraud? Why might the communists have lied about Dazhai in the first place?
b How reliable do you think **A** is? Which things in **A** do you think might be untrue?
c What problems in studying modern China have been illustrated in these pages?

3 What details in **C** and **D** are almost certainly false? Design a poster of your own attacking Dazhai and showing it to be a fraud.

20 Cultural Revolution 1

C In 1965 Chairman Mao's thoughts and sayings were published in the famous 'Little Red Book'

❝*'I was very young when the Cultural Revolution began. My schoolmates and I were among the first in Beijing to become Red Guards. We believed deeply in Chairman Mao. We spent hours just shouting slogans at our teachers.'*

The same girl remembered a really freezing winter day when she and her friends made three of the teachers from their school kneel on the ground outside without their coats or gloves. After that the leader of their group who was 18 years old told them to beat the teachers. He found some wooden boards and the pupils started hitting the teachers. 'We kept on till one of the teachers started coughing up blood. Then our leader told us to stop. We felt very proud of ourselves. It seemed very revolutionary.'❞ **(A)**   *(Told to an American reporter in China)*

What would you do if the government told teenagers to rebel against their teachers and their parents? How would you feel about teenagers taking over the country? Do you think they would make a better job of things than adults? This is what happened in China during the Cultural Revolution. Scenes like the one in A became common. For three years millions of Chinese people lived in fear of teenagers. It was all started by Mao Zedong.

By the early 1960s Mao was worried about the future of communism in China. He thought that many Party officials were becoming too *conservative* (against change). He feared that as people in the government who had fought in the Revolution died off, the new leaders would lose interest in the aims of communism. There was a danger that future Party officials and also the ordinary people of China might forget about what the Revolution had been fought for. Instead, they would only be interested in looking after their own concerns. Mao believed this was what had happened in the USSR.

To stop this happening in China, Mao decided that the People's Liberation Army and millions of young people must learn everything possible about his communist theories. They must always think about communist aims so they would be able to teach Mao's theories to the rest of the Chinese people. Also, they could then hunt out anyone who might be 'conservative' or against the aims of communism.

From 1965 onwards thousands of American soldiers

F Chairman Mao speaking to a rally in Tienanmen Square, Beijing

were being sent to fight against communism in Vietnam. The Chinese government feared that these forces might be turned against the People's Republic. This was another reason for seeking out those in China who might be against communism. Mao wanted soldiers and young people to become the defenders of the Revolution. The drive to 'educate' the people about Mao's theories and the hunting down of people who might be against communism was to be like another revolution – a Cultural Revolution.

On 1 June 1965 Lin Biao, now Minister of Defence, got rid of all ranks in the PLA. All soldiers were given a copy of the newly published *Quotations of Chairman Mao*, known as *The Little Red Book*. Lin Biao wrote in the introduction:

Comrade Mao Zedong is the greatest Marxist of our age. He has defended and developed Marxism with genius. Mao's thought is a powerful weapon for opposing conservatives. It is the guide for all the work of the Party, the army and the country. (**B**)

Photograph C shows Mao and Lin Biao with members of 'Thought Propaganda Teams', waving copies of the Little Red Book.

In August 1966 Mao announced on the radio that there were

People within the Communist Party who are in important positions and who are really capitalists. (**D**)

Liang Heng, then a 12-year-old boy living in Changsha, remembers what happened next:

Chairman Mao puts up his famous 'Bombard the headquarters' poster. He attacked the leaders from the top downwards. His main targets were Liu Shaoqi and Deng Xiaoping, the General Secretary of the Communist Party. Soon lots of local people in Changsha, some very important, were being accused and removed from office. It seemed that every day good people were being exposed as evil, and only pretending to support the Revolution. Most people felt that the Cultural Revolution was a wonderful thing because when our enemies were uncovered China would be much safer. So I felt excited and happy and wished I could do something to help. (**E**)

Liu Shaoqi and Deng Xiaoping were removed from their jobs. Deng was sent to Jiangsu where he became a waiter. Liu went to prison, where he became ill and died in 1969.

Liang soon got his chance to help (see **E**). In August 1966 Mao told students in schools and colleges to form *Red Guard* units. He wanted these Red Guards to seek out teachers who might be against communism. He also told them to go into factories and offices and into the countryside looking for officials who might not be true communists. All schools and colleges were closed so that pupils might take part in 'revolutionary activity'. Many were to stay closed for the next three years.

Mao's wife Jian Qing organised huge meetings of Red Guards in Tienanmen Square in Beijing. **F** shows one of these meetings. By the end of 1966 eight meetings had been held, attended by 11 million Red Guards. Liang Heng went to a meeting held in 1968. His account is evidence of what they were like:

Tienanmen Square was a human sea of red and green. There

were big red billboards, red balloons, red armbands, red flags, red books and red buttons. All were wearing green. While we were waiting each group sang revolutionary songs, each one trying to show greater love for the Chairman and stronger belief in communism.

Chairman Mao's car came first. As in a dream I saw him. He seemed very tall to me, truly great and larger than life. The soldiers lining the road stood at attention, but tears poured down their faces. Even so, the people nearly mobbed the car. The Chairman got out and shook hands with as many people as he could.

The fireworks were more splendid than any I had ever seen. And with every burst the hearts of tens of thousands of young people opened, showing their joy for the blessing Chairman Mao had given them. For these young people were working to save China. The last rocket burst into the words: 'Long live our great leader Chairman Mao.'* (G)

Between 1966 and 1969 the Red Guards took the law into their own hands. In many areas they carried out search raids on people's homes to see if they had anything that might show them to be against communism. Liang Heng remembers a search raid on his family's home before he became a Red Guard:

*It was a time of terror because every night we heard the sounds of loud knocks, things breaking and children crying. We knew the Red Guards would one day come to our house. At 11 o'clock one night the knocks finally came, loud and sharp. We sat up at once.

There were seven or eight of them, all men or boys. They were all wearing white cloths over their mouths and noses and dark clothes. Their leader carried a whip. He struck it against the table with a loud crack.

'Liang Shan', he said, 'Is there anything feudal, capitalist or anti-communist in your house?'

Father stammered: 'No, no. I had some pictures of Liu Shaoqi but I turned them in. Nothing else.'

'Pig!' The man sliced the table again. 'What you must understand is that this is a revolutionary action. Right?' said the man.

'Yes, yes, a revolutionary action'. I had never seen my father plead with anyone before.

'You welcome it, don't you! Say it!'

My father didn't answer.

'Shit!' You've always been a liar!' Two Red Guards took him by each arm and grabbed his head, pushing it so that he was forced to kneel down. They shook him by the hair so that his glasses fell off.

The others were already starting to go through our things. Then one of them cried out that he had found two western-style ties and a western-style jacket. 'What's the meaning of this?'

'Ties', my father mumbled. They kicked him:

'Ties! Do you think we are children? These are capitalist ties!'

Father tried to say something. The whip slammed down on his hand and he cringed in pain . . .

From the other room came two Red Guards with armfuls of books. They dumped them on the floor — old Chinese poetry, history books and Chinese legends. They burned the books where they were. Everything we owned was in a mess on the floor. Even our pillows had been slit open with a knife. The next day we found they had also taken all of Father's money.* (H)

All over China books were burned, works of art were destroyed, temples and churches were wrecked. Those suspected of being 'capitalist-roaders' (against communism) were put on trial. Some were executed. Others lost their jobs or went to prison.

Some people did not get a trial at all. Lao She, for instance, a famous Chinese writer, was simply held head down in a muddy pond by Red Guards, till he drowned. A million people died during the Cultural Revolution.

By early 1967 law and order had completely broken down in many parts of China. Things got much worse when rival Red Guard units started fighting each other. Some parts of China were now close to civil war.

??????????????

1 a Why was Mao Zedong so worried in the early 1960s?
b Why did he think it was so important to teach the PLA and the young people of China about communist aims?
c What was the 'Little Red Book'?
d What happened to Liu Shaoqi and Deng Xiaoping?
e Why did schools and colleges close in 1966?

2 a What evidence is there in this section to suggest that to millions of people Mao Zedong's 'Thought' was becoming like a religion?
b Why do you think Mao wanted the Red Guards to start by hunting out any *teachers* who might be against communism?

3 Some historians think that Mao started the Cultural Revolution for another reason. They think he was simply trying to boost his own support. Why might he need to do this? Did he succeed?

4 How far can we trust Liang Heng's accounts (**E**, **G** and **H**)? Which parts of them may be unreliable?

5 Make a list of all the things that Red Guards are doing in **A, E, F, G,** and **H.** *Discussion*: these Red Guards are nearly all teenagers. Can you imagine *any* situation which might cause you and your class to do things like this?

21 Cultural Revolution 2

The Cultural Revolution was out of control. In January 1967 fighting broke out in Nanjing between Red Guards and local 'capitalists'. 50 people died and many more were wounded. Soon street battles were going on in other towns and cities. In Beijing the British diplomatic building was burned down. Often the fighting was between rival Red Guard units and workers' groups. The PLA was told not to interfere, but sometimes they still took sides.

News of the fighting reached the outside world, but only in recent years have we discovered just how bad it was. Liang Heng's memories are again useful evidence. In A he describes fighting in Changsha between 'Rebel' Red Guards and a rival group:

I followed some people into a school and peered into rooms where a rival group of Red Guards were being beaten with leather belts. The Rebels' hatred frightened me. Some of the prisoners seemed nearly dead and were bleeding badly. That summer things got even worse in Changsha. The Rebels began fighting among themselves. Those who had once been friends became deadly enemies and the streets of Changsha ran with blood. The Cultural Revolution no longer had anything to do with the crack down on people who were against communism. That had been forgotten. A civil war was going on with each side claiming to love Chairman Mao more than the other.

The Red Guards had guns now and more. They had grenades, machine guns, and even anti-aircraft missiles. Jiang Qing's slogan 'Attack with words. Defend with guns' had been taken to mean that all questions should be settled by force. It was really terrifying. Bullets whistled in the streets, the city shook with explosions. (A)

Even the Prime Minister, Zhou Enlai, was taken prisoner by Red Guards. He was questioned for over 48 hours. Liang tells us what happened next:

The violence had to be brought under control. In September 1967 Chairman Mao visited Hunan and other provinces. He was very worried and called for an end to the fighting and told Red Guards to hand in their weapons to the PLA. Each province was to set up Revolutionary Committees, made up of all the fighting groups, as well as Party members and representatives of the PLA. Of course the different gangs weren't simply going to stop fighting just like that. It wasn't until April 1968 that the Revolutionary Committee in Hunan was formed. The aim of the Revolutionary Committees was to attack the 'capitalists' without attacking each other. (B)

In some places the PLA was sent in to restore order. In 1968 Mao Zedong once again called on young people to take action:

We need educated young people to go down to the countryside to be re-educated by the poorer peasants. People in the towns should send their sons and daughters who have finished their primary or secondary school or finished at college to the countryside. (C)

At the same time they could teach the peasants about Mao's Thought. Sending the Red Guards to the countryside was one way of stopping the fighting. It was also a way of stopping the cities from getting any bigger. Liang Heng tells us:

The young people signed up with excitement for many reasons. Some went because they wanted to get away from home, others because they longed for something fresh and because there was nothing to do at school. Above all they went because Chairman Mao had told them to go. They were told that the peasants were waiting to give them a warm welcome. Later, after the first groups had sent back reports of what things were really like, nobody wanted to go any more, but by then they no longer had any choice in the matter. I for one was really pleased to go, although I knew we were going to an extremely poor area. I imagined how we would plough, plant and eat what we grew and be able to respect ourselves again. (D)

In fact the peasants had no use for these city students. They had difficulty growing enough food for themselves as it was. Song Mingchao, another Red Guard, remembers:

Chairman Mao said we were supposed to learn from the peasants, but the peasants didn't want anything to do with us. We couldn't understand their accents anyway. They thought we were lazy. They blamed us for eating all their food without earning it. (E)

F and G show Red Guards learning from peasants. The peasants were paid by work points (see pages 40–43). They were used to really hard labour and could earn enough work points to get by. The Red Guards were not used to hard labour. Song tells us:

We were always hungry. We scrounged in the fields, looking for sweet potatoes, roots, herbs, whatever we could find. (H)

Lu Hong was one of the first Red Guards to go to the countryside. She says:

They put me on a train for the north-east. There were 2400 other students on the train. We travelled for four days and didn't know where we were going, till they let us off at a state farm near the Soviet border. At the time I was full of

F Red Guards learning how to grow rice

patriotism and wanted to defend the motherland. Then they put us in a large room made of mud, with mud walls and mud floors. 60 people slept in one room, on platforms made of mud, straw and manure. After getting up at 5 am to work in the fields, you were too tired to read at night, so some young people forgot how to read and write. (J)

Lu Hong was on the state farm for eight years. She only got away in the end because her father was an official in Peking. Many students were shocked to find out just how poor most peasants still were. Liang Heng tells us:

The peasants' day-to-day life was miserably cruel. Where was the 'Liberation' from suffering that the Revolution was meant to have given them? (K)

They were also surprised to discover that many peasants still had strong religious beliefs. Millions of peasants worshipped their ancestors. In many cases they prayed to Mao Zedong in the same way. In all, 18 million young people were sent to the countryside, about 10 per cent of all the people in Chinese towns and cities.

By 1969 the Cultural Revolution had come to an end, although it was not officially called off until after Mao's death. To millions of Chinese people Mao was a god-like figure. Lin Biao, Mao's loyal follower, was now seen as the second most important person in China. Mao's opponents in the Communist Party, such as Deng Xiaoping, had been removed.

A great deal of damage had been done during the Cultural Revolution. Industrial production had fallen. 100 million young people missed part of their education. In 1981 the New China News Agency pointed out that there were 140 million people in China who could not read or write. 120 million of them were under 45. Lu

G A group of Red Guards listening to an old peasant

Hong points out:

'I spent eight years fanning the flames of revolution. It was like losing a big chunk out of your life. Now I would like to help the motherland, but what do I have? I never finished my schooling. It's like my friends say, the Chinese people don't live, they just exist.' **(L)**

Many millions of people who suffered during the Cultural Revolution lost all respect for the Communist Party. In 1980 a 16-year-old girl told the reporter Fox Butterfield:

'The Cultural Revolution was really a good thing. In the 1950s the Chinese were very simple. They believed in the communists – like my mother. She's a teacher. Whatever the communists said she thought was great. Then in the Cultural Revolution they locked her up for a year and a half because her father was a well-known scholar whom they said was a 'capitalist'. Some Red Guards in her school made her kneel on broken glass in front of all the students. For an intelligent person it was about the worst thing that could happen – to be made to feel so small. Her eyes were opened by the Cultural Revolution. She saw through the communists.' **(M)**

The Chinese people lost out in other ways. Liao Mosha, a Communist Party author imprisoned by Red Guards for 13 years, wrote in 1980:

'When old comrades get together we often talk about the books we miss, books that have been forbidden, books that have been destroyed. Books carefully collected in libraries that have been stolen or ruined. The 'Great Cultural Revolution' was the great revolution that sent culture to its death!' **(N)**

Many educated Chinese people killed themselves because of the Red Guard actions.

??????????????

1 a What happened in January 1967 to show that the Cultural Revolution was out of control?
b Why were the red guards in Changsha fighting each other?
c What does **A** tell us about the scale of some of the fighting?
d According to **C** and **D**, how did the government bring the red guards under control again?
e Why did the red guards agree to go off to the countryside?

2 What problems did the students face in the countryside? Why was this?

3 The Cultural Revolution had a number of damaging results. What were they? Put them in order with the most damaging at the top and the least damaging at the bottom.

4 What do you think is going on in **F** and **G**?

22 Tibet

In 1950 Chinese armies invaded Tibet (see map inside front cover). There were over two million Tibetans. They had their own language, their own way of life and their own religion. Tibetans are Buddhists, and most of them believed that their ruler, the Dalai Lama (see **A**), was a god. In 1950 a third of all Tibetan men were monks. Nearly all of the most beautiful buildings in Tibet were monasteries and temples. The *feudal* life of Tibet had hardly changed for 1500 years. In theory all land was owned by the Dalai Lama. The ordinary people were mainly peasant farmers or nomads.

A The Dalai Lama

Chinese rulers, including the new communist government, had always said that Tibet was part of China. Heinrich Harrer was a friend of the Dalai Lama. He was in Tibet when the Chinese invaded:

Men prayed to the gods and looked for omens. Most people believed that a miracle would save the country from war. The Dalai Lama knew how serious things were but still hoped for peace . . . On 7 October 1950 the enemy attacked the Tibetan border in six places at once. The Chinese advanced hundreds of miles into Tibet. The Tibet National Assembly appealed to the United Nations for help . . . Their appeal was rejected. The UN said it hoped that China and Tibet could come to a peaceful agreement. In fact the Chinese troops behaved well. Tibetans who were taken prisoner later said how well they were treated. (**B**)

The Dalai Lama and his government fled from Tibet. Heinrich Harrer went with them. He tells us:

The Reds were very anxious to have the Dalai Lama back in Tibet. At last the Dalai Lama had no choice but to accept the conditions of the Chinese and return to Lhasa (the capital of Tibet). After a long time a treaty was worked out. Under this the Dalai Lama was allowed to rule the country and the Chinese government promised that there would be religious freedom in Tibet. In return Tibet had to accept that Chinese soldiers would now be in charge of the defence of the country . . .

As I write (1957) . . . there is famine in the land, which can't feed the Chinese occupying armies as well as the Tibetan people. In western newspapers I have seen Mao posters stuck up all over Lhasa, even on holy places. Armoured cars roll through the holy city. The Dalai Lama is now only a figurehead, he has no power. The Chinese have already built roads right across the trackless land to connect it with their own country. (**C**)

In 1958 the Tibetans rebelled. In 1959 the Chinese Ambassador in Lhasa was stoned to death. The Tibetan government declared Tibet independent. Chinese troops smashed the rebellion. Once more the Dalai Lama fled from Tibet into India. In the next few years he was followed by over 90 000 Tibetan refugees. The Beijing government demanded that the Indian government return the Dalai Lama, but President Nehru of India refused.

Look at map **D**. One of the roads that the Chinese built to link Tibet with the rest of China went across Aksayqin. The Indian government claimed that this was

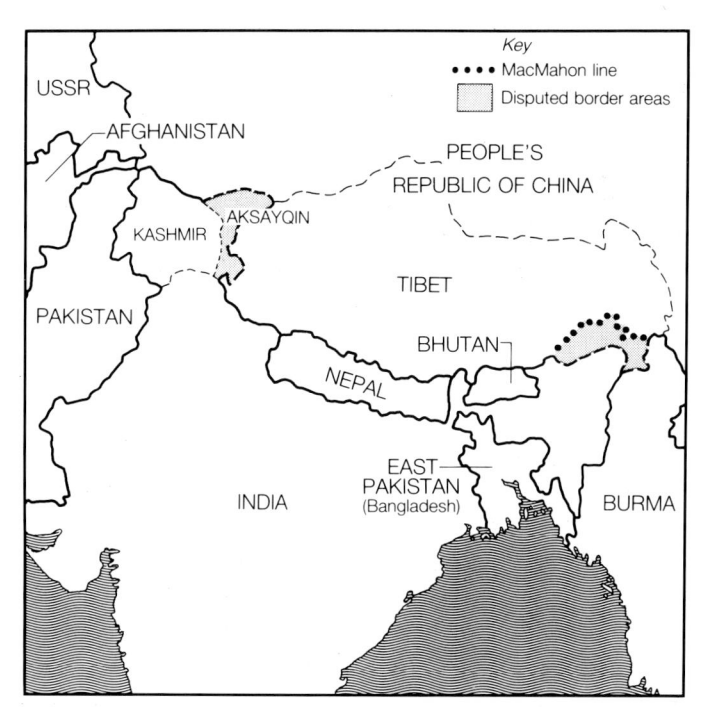

D The disputed border areas between China and India

part of India. They also said that the eastern border between India and China should be the Macmahon line, but the Chinese said the border was further south. Zhou Enlai told Nehru that he would agree to the Macmahon line if India would accept that Aksayqin was part of China. Nehru refused to agree to this.

In 1962 fighting broke out along the eastern and western borders. The Chinese troops advanced quickly and the Indians were easily beaten. The Chinese withdrew to the north of the Macmahon line, but they stayed in Aksayqin.

After the war Tibetan refugees continued to cross into India. They said that the Tibetan religion and way of life were under attack. There were reports of temples being closed, of monks being made to work in the fields and of people who spoke out against the Communist Party being put in prison. In 1965 Tibet officially became an 'Autonomous Region of China'. This meant it was self-ruling, but in fact it made little difference.

In 1966 the Cultural Revolution hit Tibet. Thousands of Red Guards arrived. They destroyed monasteries and imprisoned or killed many thousands of monks. Holy statues and other religious objects were used to make pavements and toilets. Libraries were burned to the ground.

In 1979 the Beijing Government admitted that mistakes had been made during the Cultural Revolution, which would now be put right. Communist Party leaders point out that most Tibetans are now better off than they were before 1950. They have better clothing, better housing, more food and more schools. However, parts of Lhasa lie in ruins. Of the 300 monasteries that existed there in 1950 only 13 are left. There are 500 000 Chinese now living in Tibet. Over 150 000 of them are soldiers. In 1979 John Fraser, a Canadian reporter, was allowed to visit Tibet. He pointed these things out to his guide, who replied:

'They have freedom to live their own way of life, to speak their own language, to believe what they want, to wear their own national clothes, to be educated in their own schools . . . What is more every Tibetan has a chance now to take part in the larger national life of China.' He believed this too! We were talking in Tibet where, for the most part, he and I had seen exactly the same things and come to exactly the opposite conclusions. **(E)**

Since 1979 the Beijing Government has been asking the Dalai Lama to return to Tibet. So far he has refused to go. In 1984 he said:

There are 1000 million Chinese. If something good happens there it could have a great effect. But at the moment they are causing Tibet's suffering. The real cause of the suffering is China's ignorance, greed and desire for power. **(F)**

Heinrich Harrer has written:

My greatest wish is that some understanding may grow for a people whose longing to live in peace and freedom has won so little sympathy from an uncaring world. **(G)**

??????????????

1 a In what ways was the Dalai Lama important to the people of Tibet?
b According to **B** what did the Tibetans do when they knew they were about to be invaded?
c What did the United Nations do when the Tibet government asked them for help? Why do you think this was?
d Why did fighting break out between Chinese and Indian soldiers in 1962?

2 Use the evidence on these pages to say how life has changed in Tibet since 1950. Do you agree with what the Dalai Lama says in **F**?

3 In what ways does Heinrich Harrer try to win the support of the reader in **B**, **C**, and **H**?

4 As though you are a student in a *Chinese* school or college learning about Tibet in one of your history lessons, write a short history of Tibet starting with the 'liberation' of 1950. Use *some* of the evidence on these pages to help you.

23 China and the USSR

In 1950 the People's Republic of China and the USSR made a Treaty of Friendship (see pages 38–39). Mao had said this treaty would be *'everlasting and could never be destroyed'*. 15 years later China and the USSR had become bitter enemies. The communist world is now split in two. These pages look at how and why this happened.

Soon after the Treaty of Friendship was made the Korean War broke out. In June 1950 North Korea, which the USSR backed, invaded South Korea, an ally of the USA. A United Nations force (mainly American) under US General MacArthur was sent to South Korea. It was very successful. MacArthur's army went on to invade North Korea. The Chinese Government feared this might lead to an invasion of China itself. They warned MacArthur to advance no further, but soon American soldiers had reached the border with China. In November 1950, 300 000 Chinese soldiers crossed the Yalu River into North Korea and drove back the UN forces. The fighting was very fierce. One US marine remembers:

It was like throwing pebbles at rollers in the surf. They didn't care if they were killed. (A)

Temperatures were often minus 20°C. Thousands of soldiers on both sides died of the cold. At first the

B Refugees boarding a train to escape from Korea

C   Korean War: killed and wounded

South Korea : 300 000 soldiers
United Nations : 142 000 soldiers
Chinese and North Korean :   150 000 soldiers*
Korean civilians : 1 000 000*
*(Based on United Nations estimates.)

Chinese army was so successful that US President Truman and General MacArthur even discussed using atom bombs against the Chinese. Instead the UN forces started a big counter-attack. The war dragged on until 1953. **B** shows refugees fleeing from the war. **C** shows the numbers of people killed or badly wounded.

As a result of the Korean War the People's Republic was not allowed to join the United Nations. Instead the Guomindang government in Taiwan was accepted by the UN as the official government of China. The Korean War made the friendship between the USSR and the People's Republic stronger: they were united against a common enemy. **D** is a Russian poster.

In 1953 Stalin died and Nikolai Krushchev became the new Soviet leader. Mao wrote in the *People's Daily*:

Everyone knows that Comrade Stalin had a great love for the Chinese people and believed in the mighty Chinese Revolution. He gave his great wisdom to helping with the problems of revolution. It was by following the theories of Lenin and Stalin and with the support of the great Soviet Union that the Chinese Communist Party and the Chinese people a few years ago won their historic victory. (E)

It is difficult to know how far Mao really meant this. In 1962 he pointed out:

In 1945 Stalin refused to permit China to carry out a revolution. He told us: 'Support Chiang Kaishek and do not have a civil war, for the Republic of China will fall apart.' However we did not obey him and the revolution succeeded. Even after the success of the revolution Stalin feared that China might try to be too independent of the USSR. I went to Moscow and we signed the Treaty of Friendship. This was also the result of a struggle. Stalin did not wish to sign the Treaty, he only signed it in the end after two months of negotiations. (F)

It may be that even in the early 1950s the Chinese did not fully trust their Soviet allies. After all, the USSR had supported the Guomindang in the 1920s and had given little help to the Communists during the civil wars in China. In fact Stalin had kept diplomatic relations with the Guomindang right up until 1949.

When Krushchev visited Beijing in 1954 it seemed that the two countries were still united. Krushchev promised the Chinese more loans and also help in developing nuclear power. The first sign of a split came in 1956 when Krushchev began to attack most of what Stalin had done. He said that Stalin had betrayed communism. In China Stalin was still seen as an important Marxist, even if he had been wrong about some things. Worse still, in 1957 Krushchev announced that he wanted better relations with the USA. He thought that capitalist and communist countries could live together in peace. Chinese leaders came to believe that the USSR was no longer interested in spreading communism. Soviet leaders thought that China was all too ready to face a nuclear war. They may have been right to think this. Mao wrote in the *People's Daily*:

D 'Glory to the great Chinese people who have gained freedom, independence and happiness'

❝ *I talked about the danger of nuclear war with a foreign leader* (probably Nehru, the Indian Prime Minister). *He believed that if a nuclear war were fought the whole of mankind would be killed. I said that if the worst came to the worst and half of mankind died the other half would remain while capitalism would have been smashed and the whole world would become communist. In a number of years there would be 2700 million people again and the population would still be growing. We Chinese have not yet finished building up our country and we want peace. However if the capitalist countries force a war on us we will have no choice but to fight to the finish.* ❞ (G)

After 1958 Krushchev refused to give the Chinese any more help in developing nuclear power. In 1963 China refused to sign the Nuclear Test Ban Treaty in Moscow, which had been agreed on by the USA and USSR. In 1964 the Chinese tested their own atom bomb. By this time China and the USSR were enemies.

In 1958 Mao had started the Great Leap Forward. He said that communes were 'a short cut to communism'. The Chinese were now no longer copying Soviet methods (see pages 38–39), they were building communism in their own way. To the Soviet leaders it seemed that the Chinese were breaking away from the correct path to communism. They said that Mao and other Chinese leaders were not really Marxists. In August 1960 the USSR suddenly ended all aid to China and brought back all the Russian scientists and other experts from the People's Republic.

Great industrial projects in China were suddenly brought to a standstill. The Chinese did not have enough of their own scientists to carry on with these projects themselves. Moreover when the Soviet experts left they took with them all the blueprints (plans) for these projects. This was a real setback for Chinese industry. A war of words began between the USSR and the People's Republic, with each country claiming that the other was not truly communist and each claiming to be the leader of the communist world. This hostility has gone on ever since.

China and the USSR share a border of 4500 miles. Since the early 1960s there have been many border disputes. For instance in 1969 fighting broke out along the Ussuri River, when, on the orders of Lin Biao (the Chinese Minister of Defence), Chinese soldiers ambushed a Soviet border patrol. There were also serious clashes between border soldiers in 1974 and 1978.

Since the early 1960s the Chinese have been preparing for a possible invasion by the USSR. Malcolm MacDonald, the British diplomat, remembers a conversation he had with Zhou Enlai in 1971:

J   Chinese underground shelters

'Zhou told me that in recent years relations between the two great communist nations had got even worse. The Russians have become enemy number one . . . The Chinese thought the Russians might start an attack while the People's Republic is still fairly weak. Zhou told me that this fear was backed up by the fact that the Russians have placed vast numbers of armed troops and equipment along the border.

Chinese generals were now planning to defend China in the event of a Russian, rather than an American invasion. Fear of a Russian attack was the reason for the building of air raid shelters in all parts of the country . . . every factory, school, town and city district, and almost every village in the countryside now had such shelters . . . for the same reason the army, navy and airforce were always on the alert, while the people's militia (soldiers) were constantly being trained. The government believed that all the Chinese people must be ready to fight wherever the enemy might attack. I have seen evidence of this: at a middle school I visited I watched boys and girls being taught how to throw hand grenades . . . in time of war the Russians might be able to quickly conquer whole provinces. So every province is being made self-supporting in mining, heavy industry, farming, grain storage and other needs.' (H)

K   Border patrols on China's north-west frontier

J is a drawing of the kind of shelters that have been built. K shows PLA soldiers on border patrol. In 1970 the Chinese joined the space age when they sent their first satellite into space. Chinese satellites are probably used mainly for military purposes.

In the 1980s many experts believe that a war between the USSR and the People's Republic is as likely as a war between the USA and USSR.

??????????????

1 a Why was the Chinese government worried about the UN force invading North Korea?
b What did American leaders talk about doing to stop the Chinese advance in Korea?
c According to **A**, why were so many Chinese soldiers killed?
d How does what Mao says in **F** go against what he says in **E**?

2 Draw up a chart to show how relations between China and the USSR got better or worse in: 1949, 1950, 1954, 1956, 1960, 1964, 1969, 1974, 1978.

3 Look at **J**. These kinds of shelters are now common all over China.
a What is there to show that these shelters are not just for air raids?
b What other kinds of attacks might they be used for?
c What is there to suggest that people might stay in the shelters for a long time?

4 *Either* Design a cartoon about the split between China and the USSR
Or Design a poster about defending China from attack.

24 The Other Chinas

To Chinese communists the 'liberation' of China is not finished. Hong Kong and Taiwan are not yet part of the People's Republic. Macao remains a Portuguese colony.

Hong Kong Island and the Kowloon Peninsula became British in 1842 (see pages 6–7). Hong Kong is a rich trading and banking centre with a population of five million. In 1997 Britain's lease expires and Hong Kong will become part of the People's Republic. The British have agreed to hand over Hong Kong Island and the Kowloon Peninsula as well.

The reuniting of Taiwan with Communist China is a more difficult problem. Until 1971 most western countries recognised the Guomindang government in Taiwan as the 'official' government of all China. Taiwan was a member of the United Nations. The PRC was not.

In 1949 Chiang Kaishek and about two million Guomindang supporters fled to Taiwan. Since then the communists have feared that a USA-backed invasion might be started from Taiwan. These fears increased in 1965 when US troops were sent to Vietnam. Zhou Enlai said:

'The USA could have built up big bases in Vietnam and then launched an all-out attack on China, while the Guomindang invaded from Taiwan.' (A)

The Chinese sent weapons to the communist North Vietnamese and helped train their soldiers. In fact the Guomindang has never been strong enough to invade. There are 18 million people living in Taiwan, and 1000 million in mainland China.

The USA gave a lot of money to Taiwan. Compared with mainland China it is very rich. However, as table B shows, the two countries are alike in many ways.

When China and the USSR became enemies Zhou Enlai turned to the USA. In July 1971 the US Secretary of State, Henry Kissinger, visited Beijing. After this the USA agreed to the People's Republic joining the UN. When China joined on 25 October 1971 Taiwan left the organisation. In February 1972 US President Richard Nixon visited China. He was followed by the leaders of many western 'capitalist' countries.

But China is no closer to 'liberating' Taiwan. In 1979 the Chinese National People's Congress sent this message to the Taiwan Government:

'If we do not quickly set about ending our country's division,

B The Chinese Republics

The Republic of China (Taiwan)	The People's Republic of China
1 Ruled by one party: the Guomindang	1 Ruled by one party: the Communist party
2 Trades unions are strictly controlled	2 Trades unions are strictly controlled
3 Sun Yatsen is seen as the father of modern China	3 Sun Yatsen is widely respected
4 Powerful secret police	4 Powerful secret police
5 People who criticise the government are punished. Communists are put in prison	5 People who criticise the government are arrested and 're-educated'. In 1950s/60s Guomindang supporters were arrested and shot
6 Under land reform land was taken from landlords and given to peasants	6 Under land reform land was taken from landlords and given to peasants
7 Many peasants had small plots and remained poor. Government got peasants to share land so machines could be used	7 Many peasants had small plots and remained poor. Peasants were forced to share land so machines could be used
8 Peasants kept small private plots. Sharing all the land did not produce as much as expected	8 Peasants given back small plots. Communes did not produce as much as expected
9 Mao Zedong often called the 'Great Helmsman'	9 Chiang Chingkuo (son of Chiang Kaishek) often called the 'Great Helmsman'
10 Guomindang officials say that the people of Taiwan are free while people on the mainland are ruled by communists.	10 Communist officials say that the people of Communist China are free, while people in Taiwan are ruled by capitalists.

what can we say to our ancestors or to those who come after us? This feeling is shared by all Chinese, and who among the descendants of the Yellow Emperor (in legend the founder of the Chinese nation) wishes to be thought of as a traitor for all time!' (C)

??????????????

1 Look at **B**. As if you were a supporter of the Guomindang who fled to Taiwan in 1949, write a letter to relatives in the People's Republic telling them about life in Taiwan.

25 The Struggle for Power

During the Cultural Revolution, Zhou Enlai had managed to prevent a complete breakdown of government in China. When it was over he started to sort out the mess. He brought Deng Xiaoping back into the government to help. Both Mao and Zhou were now old men (Mao was born in 1893 and Zhou in 1898). They would not be able to rule China for much longer. Lin Biao, the Minister of Defence, was Mao's chosen successor.

On 30 September 1971 the Soviet News Agency Tass reported that a Chinese plane had crashed in Mongolia on 12 September. There were no survivors and the bodies were too badly burned to be identified, but it was clear that some of them had been shot. In Beijing the People's Daily announced that Lin had been on the plane. A was written by a Chinese Communist Party member:

On 26 June 1972 a full, detailed report of the 'Lin Biao Affair' was released . . . Zhou Enlai had learned of Lin Biao's plans to kill Mao. Lin decided to escape to the USSR. Late on the night of 12 September, so the story went, Lin Biao with his wife and son escaped on a Trident jet from Beidaihe naval airport . . . When Zhou told Mao of Lin's escape Mao took no action. After an hour the aircraft disappeared from Chinese radar screens. Shortly afterwards it crashed in Mongolia, having run out of fuel. The site of the plane crash was later searched by officials from the Chinese embassy in Mongolia. They discovered the bodies of eight men and one woman. (A)

Mao later told the British Prime Minister Edward Heath:

Lin was amongst us but now we know that all the time he was under the control of the Russians! (B)

Now there was a struggle for power in China. The Communist Party was divided over what policies should be followed in the future. Table C shows the main differences between the two sides. On one side were the *Rightists* led by Zhou Enlai and Deng Xiaoping. On the other were the *Leftists*, led by Jiang Qing and three of her supporters. They were later known as the *Gang of Four*.

By 1973 Zhou Enlai was very ill with cancer. Most of his work was being done by Deng Xiaoping. One of the last things Zhou did was to announce 'The Four Modernisations' in 1975. This was a plan for China to modernise industry, farming, defence and science.

In January 1976 Zhou Enlai died. All over China people mourned. After his death it seems that the Gang of Four, with Mao's support, were in control for a time. Newspapers began attacking Deng. Early in April 1976 there was a big demonstration in Tienanmen Square in memory of Zhou Enlai. Soon it turned into a protest against the Gang of Four and in support of Deng Xiaoping. The *People's Daily* reported:

A handful of enemies of the people, pretending to remember the late Zhou Enlai, held a violent demonstration in Tienanmen Square. They put up a sign supporting Deng. Most of the people in the Square simply came to see what was going on — about 100 000 in all. A dozen young people were beaten up by some bad elements . . . The masses were really angry and said: 'We will not allow such anti-revolutionary events to take place here!' . . . But they were overcome by the few bad elements . . . Some even threw knives at the people's police . . . These people, supporters of Deng Xiaoping, wanted to bring back capitalism in China.

But they were going against the will of the people. The ordinary people, together with the people's police and army guards now moved bravely against these bad elements. Hours later thousands of people's police and PLA guards moved in to take strong measures and enforce the rule of the working-class. The bad elements could not stand against this. They squatted down like stray dogs. Some tried to fight. They were punished on the spot. (D)

On 7 April 1976 the Central Committe of the Communist Party announced:

Our great leader Chairman Mao proposed that Deng Xiaoping be sacked from all his posts and all voted in favour of this. Chairman Mao also proposed that comrade Hua Guofeng be made Acting Prime Minister. The Central Committee agreed to this. (E)

On 9 September Mao Zedong died. His body was preserved in a crystal coffin (see F). It can still be seen in Tienanmen Square in the Chairman Mao Zedong Memorial Hall. Hua Guofeng became Chairman of the Communist Party.

In October the Gang of Four were suddenly arrested. They were accused of plotting to take over the country and of trying to murder Mao Zedong. They were blamed for all that had happened in the Cultural Revolution.

In 1977 Deng was brought back into the government as Deputy Prime Minister. It was soon clear that he was now in charge, not Hua Guofeng. In 1981 the Gang of

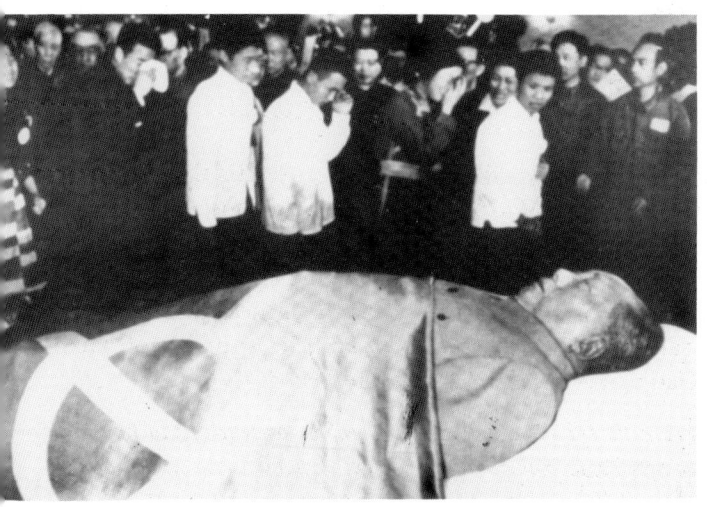

F Thousands of people filed past the body of Mao Zedong as it lay in state

Four were put on trial. They faced 48 charges. All four were found guilty and sent to prison. Jiang said at her trial:

'I was Mao's dog, whoever he told me to bite, I bit!' (G)

The trial was watched on TV all over China. One of the millions who watched it pointed out to a foreign reporter (in private):

'Everyone knows it was really Mao who gave the orders during the Cultural Revolution and it is he who should be on trial!' (H)

Deng's aim was to try to modernise China as quickly as possible, carrying on Zhou's Four Modernisations policy. However, since 1949 China's population has gone up by 450 million people. The Chinese know that unless their population stops growing, rather than becoming a modern country China will be the poorest country on Earth.

??????????????

1 a According to **A** what had Lin Biao tried to do?
  b Can we trust either **A** or the TASS report?
  c What evidence is there to suggest that Lin may have been murdered?

2 Which parts of **D** do you think are unlikely to be true? What reasons might the *People's Daily* have for lying?

3 This obituary was written about Chairman Mao:
'Chairman Mao led our party, our army and the people of our country in using people's war against the rule of foreigners, feudalism and capitalism. He blazed a new trail for the cause of freedom of the enslaved peoples of the world.'
What do *you* think of Mao Zedong? Write your own obituary on him.

The struggle for power

THE LEFT The Gang of Four	THE RIGHT Zhou Enlai and Deng Xiaoping
1 Communist China's way of life is better than any other country's. The Chinese Revolution must be kept going at any cost.	1 China is backward compared with the rest of the world. Most people still live in poverty.
2 China's population is so big she can resist any invasion. China's people must be trained to fight 'a people's war'.	2 China's weapons are out-of-date. She must get new, modern arms in case of war with the USSR.
3 All Chinese people must follow Mao Zedong's thought. When they are united they will be able to overcome all problems. Trade with western countries could lead to a return of capitalism.	3 China lacks the technology and money to modernise industry. She must seek help from western capitalist countries. They will be able to provide scientific knowledge and start industrial projects.
4 Food production has not gone up fast enough because peasants still own their own land. If peasants share land they will all work harder.	4 Because all land is owned by communes peasants have no reason to work hard. Land should be divided among peasants to farm as they like.
5 All workers should be paid the same – that is one of the aims of Communism.	5 There should be bonuses and promotion for workers to encourage everyone to work harder.
6 The Party must remain in total control. Otherwise its enemies may start up capitalism again.	6 There must be less Party interference in industry and farming. Peasants know best what to grow, factories should choose what to produce.

26 China's Population

*'My mummy had only one.
We don't want brothers or sisters.
Everyone is happy!
The whole house rejoices!'* (A)

A is a new children's song taught in Chinese infant schools. In 1980 the government announced:

'... it is necessary to start a special programme to control our population growth. In future all couples may only have one single child each.' (B)

Chinese leaders want the One-Child Policy to last for 100 years. In 1949 there were about 540 million people in China (including Taiwan, Macao and Hong Kong). By 1982 the population had nearly doubled to over 1000 million people. If it continues to grow at that rate then early in the 21st century hundreds of millions of Chinese people could face starvation. Although food production has also doubled, a government official points out:

'In 1977 grain production per head of population was the same as it was in 1955. That is, the growth in grain production was only about equal to the growth in population . . .' (C)

The Chinese have always had large families. People in country areas want to have children who will look after them when they are old. The main reason why the population has grown so quickly is that the infant mortality rate (number of babies who die before the age of one) has dropped sharply. This is a result of better health care, better housing and better food distribution since 1949. The 1982 Chinese census found that two-thirds of China's population were below the age of 24. Chinese people are also living longer. In 1900 life expectancy (the average length of life) was about 27 years. Now Chinese people can expect to live to be 70.

In the late 1950s the government started a birth control campaign. Contraceptives became free, but this made little difference in the country areas. So in 1980 the One-Child Policy was started. When young people wish to get married they now have to get permission from their brigade family planning officer. They must take a written test in family planning and they must be over 24. Each year the brigade is told how many births it is allowed. A married couple must get permission from their brigade family planning officer to have a child, and they are only allowed one.

Many parents want more than one child. In 1982 a BBC film team weant to the 'model' town of Changzou. They spoke to a Mrs Chang. She had become pregnant for the second time, without permission. After seven months her pregnancy was discovered and she ran away to her mother. She told the BBC:

'My brigade leaders wanted me to come back so we could discuss whether I should have an abortion.'
Chang's family planning officer pointed out: *'When we started trying to change her mind she was seven months pregnant . . . I was very worried, seeing her get bigger and bigger . . . The leaders of the commune all came to persuade her.'*
Chang said *'I did want to have the baby but after they came and did their work I agreed to have an abortion.'*
The family planning officer went on: *'We thought it would be best for her if she was sterilised, but at first she would not agree . . . In the end I talked her round to being sterilised.'* (D)

Married women are asked to sign a One-Child Contract, or 'Glory Certificate' promising that they will only have one child. Mrs Tian, another family planning officer, tells us:

'For those who agree . . . there is a package of rewards: a monthly bonus of five Yuan (about £2) for each parent until the child reaches 14. (This is about 8 per cent of a town worker's average pay.) The child will also get the best schooling and the parents get the right to better housing. Each brigade has women officials to keep an eye on the women and look out for any signs of pregnancy. There is no room for personal freedom on such an important issue!' (E)

The parents of the child also become 'model workers'. If all workers in a brigade sign the Glory Certificate it becomes a model brigade and all the members get extra bonuses. One factory official told the BBC:

'We have managed to gain the so-called 'three withouts': Without permission no-one is pregnant. We are without any second child. We are without any under-age mothers.' (F)

G shows children in a factory nursery. If a woman breaks her One-Child Contract she has to pay back all the benefits. When they have had their one child, either the husband or wife is asked to be sterilised. Ten times more women than men end up being sterilised.

In the countryside there has been a terrible, unexpected result of the One-Child Policy. Thousands of baby girls have been killed by their fathers. Many peasants value sons more than daughters. Girls usually

G Many factories provide nurseries where children are looked after while their parents work

leave home to get married. Also, the family name is passed through the males. The Communist Party Women's Federation sent officials to Anhui Province to get some idea of the scale of the problem. In 1983 they reported:

‹ 1 In some parts of Anhui Province there are five times as many male as female babies. 2 In one village more than 40 babies had been drowned in the past two years. 3 In another village eight babies had been born in the last year. Three boys were still alive. Three girls had been drowned and two girls had been abandoned. 4 In the whole of Anhui for every 100 girls under the age of one there were 111 boys. 5 Unknown numbers of women had been beaten by their husbands for giving birth to a girl instead of a boy. › (H)

Even if the One-Child Policy works there will still be an extra 200 million Chinese people in the year 2000. If the policy works for 100 years, as Chinese leaders hope, the population is expected to drop to about 600 million. As **J** shows, China could face disaster if the policy does not work. Chinese people can only just grow enough food as it is. In the 1970s drought or floods meant big food shortages and famine in Anhui, Henan, Shandong, Jiangsu and Sichuan. One family planning officer pointed out:

‹ Personally I feel for people who want more than one child . . . But in the interests of the country we can't let them have a second one. If one couple have two many others will want a second and that would make our work impossible. › (K)

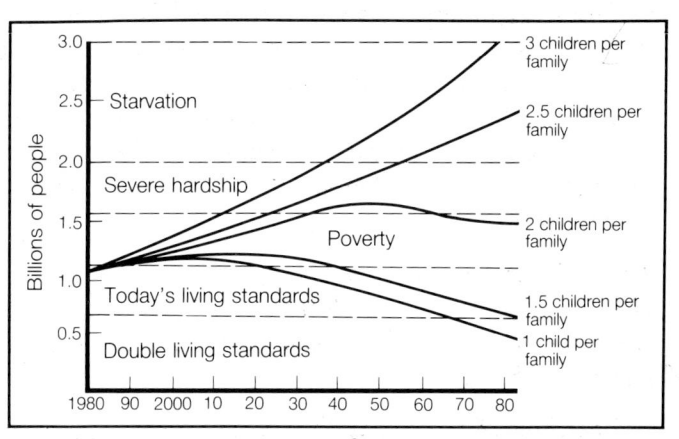

J Chinese government forecasts on the effects of population growth by 2080

???????????????

1 a By how much did China's population grow each year between 1949 and 1982? Why did this happen?
b Why did free contraception fail to solve the problem?
c What do all couples have to do before they are allowed to marry?
d Why are thousands of baby girls being killed?

2 Use the evidence to explain how the government is trying to make people follow the One Child Policy. Which of the methods do you agree with?

3 What evidence is there on these pages to suggest that women are still far from equal to men in modern China?

4 Do *You* agree with the One-Child Policy? Find out what other members of your class think of it. Try to persuade them round to your point of view.

27 Modern China

Chinese production continued to grow in the 1960s and 1970s, despite the setbacks caused by the Great Leap Forward, the Cultural Revolution and the Gang of Four. On 8 March 1978 Deng Xiaoping (A) told the Chinese Science Conference:

In ancient times China had very great achievements in science. It played a big part in the advance of the world. This can only make us more confident about catching up with and overtaking the advanced countries of the world. China must with energy follow the Four Modernisations of farming, industry, defence and science. This does not mean shutting the door on the world or blindly opposing all that is foreign. (B)

In 1978 the Chinese made a Treaty of Peace and Friendship with Japan. In 1979 the USA and China began 'normal' relations. In 1979 Deng toured the USA and signed trade agreements with President Jimmy Carter, while Hua Guofeng went to Western Europe.

The Four Modernisations can only work with the help of the West's modern science and money. In *industry* joint projects have been started with western companies. For instance US and British oil companies are now drilling for oil off the coast of China. Many western companies are now allowed to sell their goods in China. Provinces, towns and factories have been given permission to make their own agreements with foreign companies. For *defence* the Chinese have bought planes, tanks and guns from western countries. In *science* there are special training programmes for top students. By working with western companies the Chinese get the most modern equipment. To pay for this China has borrowed money from western banks and started up a big tourist industry. In *farming* the 'Responsibility System' was started in 1978. The land was divided up among peasant families and they were made responsible for it. They have to give a fixed amount of what they produce to the government, the rest they can sell on the open market. According to the government between 1978 and 1982 food production went up by 15 per cent. The communes have been broken up. This means that some peasants can earn much more than others. In June 1984 the *People's Daily* reported:

Peasants beat a rich peasant into a coma because they were jealous of his success. Four months after Liu Zhuquan was blindfolded and beaten with iron bars he is unable to walk or look after himself and he can't speak properly. (C)

Many people hoped that with the defeat of the Gang of Four there would be greater freedom in China. In 1978 people began sticking up posters on what became known as 'Democracy Wall', in Beijing, saying what they thought of the Gang of Four and the new government. This was allowed to go on for several months before there was a clamp down. Those caught sticking up posters were sent to labour camps. D is from one of these posters:

Since the defeat of the Gang of Four by our wise and great leaders, Deng and Hua, we have hoped for more democracy. To the people's regret however the hated old political system has not changed. We are not even allowed to talk about freedom and democracy. (D)

The Chinese face many other problems. In 1984 a British reporter in Beijing pointed out:

Twenty million people in Chinese cities are unemployed, or 'waiting for work' as the government puts it. Most of them are young men and many have turned to violent crime. Seven or eight thousand of them have been shot in the last six months and 750 000 have been sent to distant labour camps. (E)

Even so, the Communist Party is turning China into a 'superpower'. Chinese leaders see themselves not only as leaders of the communist world, but also as leaders of the poor countries of the world. In the 1980s the Chinese government is giving billions of pounds of aid to many African and Asian countries. In the future, what happens in China will have a bigger and bigger effect on what happens in the rest of the world. During your lifetime Beijing may well become the world's most important city. Modern China has become, and will remain, a giant of our age.

A   Deng Xiaoping